HUMBLER THAN DUST
A Retired Couple Visits the Real India
by Tandem Bicycle

PAKISTAN

New Delhi

Agra

Sawai Madhopur

Kota

Ujjain

INDIA

Calcutta

Aurangabad

Nasik

Mumbai
(Bombay)

BAY
OF
BENGAL

Hyderabad

ARABIAN
SEA

Chennai
(Madras)

—————— Segment not cycled

------ Route cycled

HUMBLER THAN DUST

A Retired Couple Visits the
Real India by Tandem Bicycle

by Mona Lee

SEABOARD PRESS

AN IMPRINT OF J. A. ROCK & CO., PUBLISHERS

Humbler Than Dust,
A Retired Couple Visits the Real India by Tandem Bicycle by Mona Lee

SEABOARD PRESS

is an imprint of *JAMES A. ROCK & CO., PUBLISHERS*

Address comments and inquiries to:
SEABOARD PRESS
James A. Rock & Company, Publishers
9710 Traville Gateway Drive, #305, Rockville, MD 20850
E-mail:
jrock@rockpublishing.com   lrock@senseofwonderpress.com
Internet URL: www.SenseOfWonderPress.com

Paperbound ISBN: 0-918736-86-2

Printed in the United States of America

First Edition: August 2005

Cover Photos property of Mona Lee.

The author would like to thank Lisa Maynard for her
help with editing this book.

This book is dedicated to the generous people of India who shared freely with us the resources, wisdom, and beauty of their culture.

Contents

CHAPTER 1

Touts and Beggars

My husband, Dick, is a handsome gray-haired mathematician with an imperturbable disposition and the well tuned body of a cyclist. However, at two AM after twenty-five hours on a passenger jet to Bombay, he looks as frazzled and confused as a robot whose wires have shorted out. Tugging our big heavy suitcase and wearing an enormous backpack, he stumbles past the booth marked, *Pre-paid taxis 650 Rupees* and steps onto the pavement outside the terminal.

I too must look as I feel, even more dazed and out of sorts than Dick. Having been a bicycle commuter before retiring from my job as a social worker, I am also normally in pretty good shape, but at this moment I am the stereotype of a senior citizen tourist, a snowy headed old lady with sagging cheeks and wrinkled brow. "Oh yes, maybe there are taxis waiting outside that charge less," I say. For our lay-over last night in Bangkok, the taxi service inside the terminal had tried to charge us twice the going rate outside.

"Our guide book says the taxi fare downtown should be three-fifty," Dick remembers. But I also recall that the book warns against touts who scam gullible tourists in numerous, creative ways like taking them to expensive hotels for kickbacks. We are both cost-conscious because we finance our *Bike for Global Democracy* trips

1

entirely from our modest pensions. We have already trained ourselves to mentally calculate the exchange rate of rupees to dollars. Six hundred fifty rupees translates to around thirteen dollars, about the price of a taxi ride from the Seattle airport to our home. However, we have been told that India would be cheaper.

The Bombay terminal with its gray, functional walls and stone tile flooring dredges up early childhood memories of bus stations during the late 1940's when the U.S. was emerging from the Depression. To reach the squat toilets in the restroom, I had stepped over women in saris asleep on the floor. Now I hesitate at the lobby exit and shuffle out with Dick into the equally uninviting street. There is no one else waiting, and there are no taxis. All is still and dark except for a couple of spotlights hanging from the edge of a building across the way.

Suddenly a man is standing in front of us, then two, then three. We can barely see them in the ambient light. The first man is chubby and wears a filthy turban wound like a dish cloth around his oily black hair and scraggly, frosted beard. The second man is even dirtier. Instead of on his head, he wears the dish cloth draped over his stomach and hanging down in front. This must be a dhoti, or sort of skirt worn by men. I remember reading about that in the guidebook. The third man has a crew cut. He wears a plain T-shirt and a pair of tattered jeans. The three of them stand abreast forming a black wall of silhouettes between us and the spotlights.

"Taxi!" says the man in the turban.

"You need hotel!" says the man in the T-shirt.

"I get taxi," insists the man in the dhoti and runs off into the dark street.

"There don't seem to be any taxis waiting here like there were in Bangkok," I say.

"We get taxi. Take you to good hotel," assures the turbaned man.

"We have reservations at Bentley's Guest House in Colaba," says Dick.

"Oh that is far. We go hotel very near."

"No, we want to go to Colaba," says Dick.

The man shakes his turban. "Long way. Cost many rupees."

"How many rupees?"

The men do not reply. They stand like silent sentries guarding us as if to prevent our escape. In fact, when I try to walk around them, the turbaned man holds out his arm like a barrier at a railroad crossing and insists, "We get you taxi!"

"Why are there no taxis in front of the terminal?" asks Dick. "Where are they?"

"Taxis not allowed waiting in terminal. Must go out for taxi."

"Then we'll go out and get one," says Dick. He tries to walk around the two men, but the man in the dhoti comes panting back. "Taxi! We have taxi!" he calls.

"How much, what cost to Colaba, three hundred fifty rupees?" Dick asks.

Without answering, the three men literally grab our luggage away from us and start running off into the darkness. We have little choice but to chase after them or lose our luggage.

About a half block down the street waits a rattle trap beige car, much like the Studebaker my Dad junked back in the fifties. The three men stuff our luggage into the trunk and open the back door, motioning for us to get in.

"Something is creepy about this," I say to Dick. We both hesitate before getting in, but what choice do we have? As far as we can tell there is no other candidate to take us to Bentley's in Colaba, and it is now past two AM. We get in slowly, our bottoms feeling metal beneath the burlap bags which serve as upholstering for this questionable rig.

"Where is the driver?" asks Dick, observing that there is no one in the driver's seat.

The turbaned man gets in. "I am driver," he says.

"This is pretty fishy," I point out.

"What cost to Colaba?" persists Dick.

"We charge night time rates, very far, very expensive." The turbaned man presses a switch to awaken a grumbling engine, and we jerk away from the terminal building.

About a quarter of a mile farther on, the terminal complex exits onto a traffic circle. There we notice a queue of taxis waiting alongside of the road. They have official black logos and look to be in far

better shape than the vehicle we're in. I figure they're probably waiting to be called from the prepaid six-fifty taxi stand inside the terminal. I want to go back and start all over using that method, but
I'm pretty sure Dick would not agree to six-fifty. "What cost to
Colaba?" he asks again.

"Tell us the cost now or take us back to the airport!" I demand,
my voice rising to crescendo.

"Long way to Colaba," says the turbaned man. He shows us a
printed fare schedule. "Night time rates. Cost is twenty-one hundred rupees."

"Take us back to the airport at once!" I shriek.

"Take us back now, or let us off right here" agrees Dick. "We
won't pay that. The prepaid cost is only six hundred fifty rupees."

"Okay, six-fifty," says the turbaned man.

"No, take us back to the airport!" I shout. I'm not about to trust
this scoundrel to take us across the street, let alone all the way to
Colaba, wherever that is.

I'm feeling pretty panicky by now. Here we are an older couple
who have clearly been targeted by scam artists because we look
bumbling and inexperienced. We are alone in a huge foreign country where we don't know more than three or four words of any native language. Our limited knowledge has been gleaned from a few
guide books and several conversations with friends before we left
our home in Seattle. Yet we are daring to take a thousand kilometer
tandem bicycle trip, launching out on our own across an unknown
land. What kind of quixotic dreamers are we anyway to presume
that we can traipse about the world promoting the idea of a global
parliament elected by the people if we can't even get a taxi from the
airport?

A retired co-worker, Rani, had grown up in India and still par-
takes almost exclusively of Indian culture within her small local immigrant community. When I told Rani we were planning a bicycle
trip in India, she said, "No! You cannot bicycle in India. That's absurd! It's out of the question!"

"Well, we're going to do it," I said. "We already have our air-
plane tickets and have told all our friends."

"You must be crazy!" she said.

"Why?"

"The roads are very bad. Trucks and buses will run you over."

Another young friend named Timothy had spent a couple of months in an ashram learning meditation from a guru. As we sipped lattes in a Seattle coffee house, Timothy had given us two pieces of advice. He said, "Remember you are a wallet, not a person." After a couple of more sips, he added, "Never expect anything to go smoothly while you're in India."

My friend Joan, another former co-worker, had taken a series of two-week trips to visit her guru. Joan's advice had been mostly medical. "Don't drink any water unless it is bottled and be sure you break the seal yourself."

"Also, make sure you get traveler's medical insurance. If something serious happens, you will want to be evacuated to a hospital in Germany. Medical care in India is very poor."

"Oh, and bring your own disposable syringes. They just wash things. They don't sterilize."

A world traveler peace activist friend named Mike had shuddered visibly and said, "India is very ugly." Then his face had relaxed into a sad smile. "Very ugly and very beautiful."

These variable claims about India had echoed through the chambers of my mind as we peered down over the wing of Northwest Flight 7 taking off from Seatac International Airport and heading out across Puget Sound. Below we could see the U.S. Naval Submarine Base at Bangor, and we even located the little green meadow with our vacation cottage overlooking Hood Canal and the snow-covered Olympic Mountains. Dick had pointed out some of our favorite hiking destinations — Quilcene, Cameron Pass, the Elwha River Valley, and Hurricane Ridge. We had such a good life in Washington State. Why were we headed off against the advice of friends to be strangers in an unknown world?

Dick's normally gentle voice is now raised to its most assertive volume. "Take us back to the airport now!" he insists.

The turbaned man drives twice around the traffic circle while trying to convince us to trust him and that he will only charge six hundred and fifty rupees.

"No! Take us back!" I reach for the door handle as if I intend to jump out onto the traffic circle.

To our relief, after the third pass around the circle, the car rumbles back toward the terminal where we get out, and the turbaned man helps us unload our luggage. By this time he is peering quizzically at us as if wondering what we plan to do next.

Actually, it had been my plan to go in and order a prepaid taxi for six hundred fifty rupees, but Dick dons his pack and begins to pull the heavy suitcase back toward the traffic circle. "There was a whole bunch of taxis along the road out there. We'll get one for three fifty," declares this brave soul.

I have no choice but to pick up my luggage and follow. Although Dick has the heaviest pieces, mine are by no means insignificant. Dick is pulling the big wheeled suitcase containing our entire disassembled *Bike Friday* custom travel tandem bicycle. What few parts he had been unable to fit into the suitcase are stored in the enormous backpack with his clothing and personal items. Most of my things are packed in a big green duffle bag which hangs down the front of my chest by a strap across my shoulder. I also wear a small backpack of books and supplies I wanted to keep handy on the plane. Dangling from each hand is a pair of bicycle panniers containing our helmets and water bottles. Sweating under the yoke of these burdens, we trudge into a strange dark world.

We have not gone far before one of the black, more official looking taxis pulls up beside us and stops. The driver jumps out. "Taxi?"

"Yes, taxi," I say.

"How much to Colaba? Three hundred fifty rupees?" says Dick.

"Four hundred."

"Let's pay four hundred," I urge, and fortunately Dick agrees.

As the taxi races through the darkened streets, I perceive Bombay as an unlikely tourist destination. The roadsides are lined with corrugated metal squares that look like small garage doors. Sometimes the taxi goes over a viaduct and I can see the upper stories of concrete or stucco apartment buildings with blackened and crumbling facades. Here and there human forms crouch over smoking fires along the street, or people sleep on blankets in the open air. Garbage, plastic bags, tin cans and paper wrappers cover every inch of ground. The air blasting my face through the open window smells like a blend of metallic smoke and sewage.

Perhaps this spectacle of pollution and litter should not come as such a shock. I should have anticipated this natural consequence of combining corporate industrialization with overpopulation and extreme poverty. After all, the relatively poor southeast Seattle neighborhood where I live is a lot more littered than wealthier suburbs. Poor people are focused on the mechanics of survival and have spare attention or resources to expend on careful disposal, let alone recycling, of coke bottles and junk food packaging.

* * * *

As I clutch Dick's arm to brave the humbling experience of sightseeing on our first day in old Bombay, we are surrounded by what were probably once magnificent streetscapes, like something out of Venice. There are pointed arches over windows and tile patterns gracing the facades of towers and onion domes. But buildings are crumbling away under improvised additions like awnings made of rusty tin roofing or deteriorating straw mats for window dressings. Ferns and saplings grow out of cracks high in the outer walls. Memory of the British occupation must be so bad that people watch gleefully as remnants of European culture crumble back into the dust.

Sightseeing is seriously hampered by the chaos of traffic. I feel that we are in a transmigration of ants besieged by an aggressive swarm of hungry beasts known as auto rickshaws. People don't walk much on sidewalks here. Instead they prance down the middle of the street, even as rickshaws and motorcycles flit every which way through, around, and about them. It's not just the engines; it's the cacophony of honking, shrieking, and trumpeting horns as well. Drivers don't form lanes here — they just swerve and honk. There needs to be a method whereby an oncoming motorist warns another that he's being overtaken, so they use their horns incessantly. I give up on my hearing aids and store them inside my pack.

This custom of sauntering down the middle of the street in the midst of chaos is perfectly plausible, given the millions of pedestrians and very little usable sidewalk space. It appears that someone, perhaps the British, back some time ago did build lots of beautiful sidewalks, graceful promenades constructed of artistic paving stones in various geometric shapes. Now most of the stones are missing as clouds of orange dust billow out into the air already heavily polluted with auto exhaust and factory smoke. These dust paths are flanked on either side by vendor stalls stacked and hung with everything from colorful silks to radios to food being deep-fried right there on the spot. If you do try and make your way down the narrow dusty path between the stalls, you are constantly pounced upon by vendors, called wallahs. "Ice cream, Madame!" "Nice pair of sandals, best quality! Good price!" At least in the middle of the street you only have to contend with traffic and can maintain a safer distance from wallahs who want your wallet.

Crossing at a busy intersection, I suddenly feel the touch of a tiny hand holding mine way down low at the end of my arm. I look down and see a little brown boy with bright pleading eyes gazing up at me. He is covered with grime, and a wad of yellow mucous runs down his nose into his mouth. He is about the size of an average North American preschooler, but there is an air of far greater sophistication about him. Startled, I pull my hand away and reach up to take hold of Dick's arm. We have already been confronted by several begging children since leaving Bentley's Guest House this morning, but this is the first one to take my hand. I want very much to give him money, even to take him home with me perhaps, but Dick says it is wrong to give money to beggars.

"If you give them money, it rewards and therefore perpetuates the system."

"So, if you don't give them money will that change the system?"

"The children are only begging because their parents make them do it. India has free public schools. Children should be in school, not begging in the street. They would be fed at school and later learn a trade."

I try to soothe my conscience with Dick's argument as a pretty little girl looks up to me with pleading eyes and calls out, "Baksheesh!" which means beggar's money. It doesn't help. What helps is doing arithmetic. With so many begging children, if I gave each of them the least acceptable donation, say a few rupees; we would have to cancel our trip. The shoe string upon which we are traveling would not stretch that far. Besides, I've been told that Hindus believe giving alms to beggars wins favor from the gods. If you give to a beggar, it's a gift to humanity. With so many Hindus around, maybe these youngsters will do a fairly brisk business without my patronage.

After lunch, we take a taxi ride over to Mani Bhavan, Gandhi's former home in Bombay, now a museum containing one of the largest collections of books and writings by and about him. Framed by one doorway is a life-sized photo of the great man wearing his simple dhoti and soft peaceful smile. The portrait is so realistic that the resurrected Mahatma appears to be striding into the library with his walking stick at this very moment. I sit at the table near his picture reading the thoughts of this grand soul and imagining a very different world transformed by a universal commitment to his teachings.

Dick, who was a conscientious objector during the Viet Nam War, shows me a copy of the book that most influenced his youth and turned him into the abstemious vegetarian peace activist that he has been ever since. The book is entitled, *Experiments in Truth, an Autobiography.* As I sit in the room that was once Gandhi's study reading the introduction to his autobiography, one quote takes hold of my mind, to say nothing of my nose, throat, and lungs, perhaps my whole being. "The seeker after truth," he says, "Must be humbler than dust. Only then and not til then will he ever have a glimpse of truth."

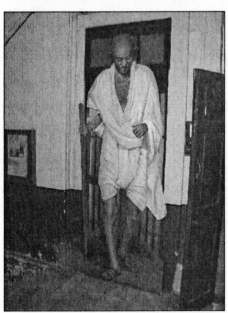

Life-sized photo of Gandhi in Mani Bhavan, his former home in Bombay.

After only half a day in India, it has become obvious to me that if anything is more omnipresent than poverty, it is perhaps dust. Drifting from broken sidewalks, hanging in the air and coagulating in the lungs, dust covers virtually everything, even the glossy leaves of the akosha trees. If you touch the petals of flowers, brownish-yellow dust rubs off on your fingers. I can feel it on my eyelashes and continually clean my fingernails to no avail. After only a few moments, they will be clogged again.

I recall a biblical quote from my Catholic childhood. "Remember man that thou art dust, and unto dust thou shalt return." It is interesting to juxtapose the two statements about dust, one by Gandhi and the other by Jesus. Together their thoughts transform dust into a symbol of the human spirit. Giving my imagination full reign, I can see dust imbued with the blended spirits of deceased humanity swirling about the streets and interacting intimately with the living world.

If anything is as omnipresent as poverty and dust in India, it is spirituality. In every stall along the street there is a miniature shrine draped with garlands and smoking with incense to honor some god or other. As for Dick and me, I suspect our spirits will grow immensely as we interact with the spiritual cultures cloaked in the humble dust of India.

Leaving Mani Bhavan, we walk along the littered Chowpatty beach looking out over the Arabian Sea, then hike up Malabar Hill, a residential street flanked by apartment buildings and the white spires of a Jain temple. Crowning the hill is the Hanging Gardens, a park with great views out over the City and the Sea. We dawdle there and watch children in a giant shoe playground gym. It looks like the shoe from illustrations of the nursery rhyme, "There was an old woman who lived in a shoe. She had so many children she didn't know what to do." That reminds me of a comment the guesthouse manager made this morning. "India has only one problem," he said. "We have too many people." Too many touts and beggars, too many homeless people living in slums that reportedly cover two-thirds of Bombay.

On our way back, we stop at one of the numerous STD stalls scattered throughout Bombay. The first time we had noticed a big STD sign over a shop across the street from Bentley's Guest House, I had remarked to Dick that perhaps it dispensed free condoms to fight AIDS. So I was amazed when I asked the guesthouse manager to use the phone, and he sent me across the street to that very shop. How naïve I was not to know that in much of the world the STD acronym does not connote "sexually transmitted disease." Rather it is a convenient technology for making long distance calls.

The phone transaction takes place in a little stall, much like any shop or store in India. Stores hardly seem to exist in terms of the four-walled buildings we have always known. Stalls typically have three walls lined with shelves and merchandise. The fourth side is open to the air with a counter across the front. Often, we're told, the proprietor sleeps inside the stall which is also his home. He probably gets breakfast from a nearby food stand. In the case of an STD stand, a machine resembling a cash register with a phone receiver, sits on the counter. The customer picks up the receiver and dials the number. The machine times the conversation and prints out the bill. It's very simple. The only technical challenge is for my hearing-aides, given the deafening street noise in the background.

I had tried several times this morning to phone Sant Dos Srivastava, a Servas host with whom we hope to stay in Agra, our next destination. Our plan is to bicycle one thousand kilometers from that city back to Bombay, arriving here in time for the World Social Forum in mid-January. But we flew into Bombay first because it was cheaper to get a round-trip ticket to the larger city and then pay for a one-way train to Agra. In Agra we hope Mr. Srivastava will help us get oriented and send us on our way bicycling back to Bombay. My attempts to reach Mr. Srivastava this morning had been greeted by buzzing noises like a busy signal. But this time when I dial the number, a young man answers.

"Are you Mr. Srivastava, a member of Servas?" I ask.

"Servas? What is that?"

I am delighted to make contact with anyone speaking intelligible English even if it *is* the wrong number. "Servas is an organization of peace activists that provide home stays for one another traveling about the world."

"Servas? No, I am not a member, but it sounds very good. I would like to belong to such a fine organization." The voice sounds pleasant and inviting.

"Oh, yes. Well do you happen to know someone named Sant Dos Srivastava? Is this number 2 25322356?"

"Mmm. Yes, that is my number, but I don't know Mr. Srivastava. However, the name sounds familiar. Does he live in Agra?"

"Yes. Have I reached Agra?"

"Yes, I am in Agra. I can try to help you find Mr. Srivastava."

"That would be great!" I say. "In a little while we have to get on the train, the Punjab Mail, and go to Agra. We will arrive tomorrow evening. We would like to stay with Sant Doss Srivastava."

"Good! You come to Agra tomorrow. When you arrive, phone me. I will help you find him."

"That's wonderful! Thank you very much, Mister . . . What is your name?"

"Gaurau Singh."

"What?" So far, my mind has never registered more than a vague concept of any Indian name from first auditory input. I don't know whether that is because of my hearing impairment, the age of my brain, my relative lack of prior experience with Asian languages, or all of the above.

"Gaurau Singh," he repeats.

"Okay." I write down "G. SING" next to a wrong number for Sant Doss Srivastava. "Thank you so much, Mr. Singh."

"You are welcome. I will meet your Punjab Mail train tomorrow evening."

While I pay for the call, Dick hails a taxi. We are off to get our luggage and head for the station.

After all we have been through with the touts of Bombay, I don't know why I have decided to trust Mr. G. Singh. For all we know, he might be another swindler with a nicer voice and a better command of English. But for lack of a viable alternative, we entertain two rays of hope, one that we will be greeted in Agra by the total stranger I have just met by phoning the wrong number, and the other that he will turn out to be a nice person.

CHAPTER 2

Escape from Victoria Station

The vast panorama inside Victoria Station looks like a mass migration from a nuclear attack. Over the central portion of the floor, hundreds of people sit or lie on blankets amongst an array of dust, bottles, and food packaging. One little boy lies alone in the dirt, not moving a muscle. His eyes are closed in complete repose, and I can't tell whether he is dead or only sleeping. No one else seems to take any notice of the child, so we hurry by, nearly stepping on him in our haste to catch the train. Above this untidy scene hangs a huge sign in twelve-inch letters ironically proclaiming in English that, *Cleanliness is next only to godliness.*

Around the outskirts of the seated masses, hundreds more people rush helter-skelter, pressing one another through doorways as they hurry to and from the trains. We edge through the crowd toward the outer platform from which we believe our train, number eleven, the Punjab Mail, is scheduled to leave in half an hour for Agra.

As we approach the platform, I notice that number eleven is lit up above the train. But to my shock and dismay, the train begins to move. The lighted number blinks off. I stop breathing as the train disappears with the speed of an arrow from its bow and is gone. I look at my watch. It says six thirty. "I thought the train was sup-

The crowds bustle outside Victoria Station in Bombay.

posed to leave at seven," I say. Dick nods toward the wall clock across the platform. There is an expression of horror on his face. "My god, it *is* seven," he moans. "We must have set our watches wrong at the airport the other night. I guess we've been a half hour off ever since."

From this moment we enter a hellish melodrama or perhaps a TV sitcom as several touts descend like hounds upon us. These swindlers have a sixth sense. They seem to know instinctively when trouble has befallen a pair of inexperienced foreigners. But I suppose it isn't difficult to spot us. We are the only westerners in sight. On top of that, we look waylaid and confused.

Even though their appearance is unlike the mangy trio that had attacked us at the airport, it's as easy for us to spot a tout as it is for them to sense our crisis. These characters are dressed in fairly clean suits and ties. Certainly they have a *lean and hungry look*, but that is not what identifies them instantly as villains. It's their relentless and forceful pursuit. If someone sincerely offers help and it is refused, the expectation would be for them to go away. Not so with touts.

No matter how often we tell them to leave us alone, no matter how persistently we ignore them, they are at our heels like dogs after their prey. I imagine a sitcom audience laughing as the touts chase us around the terminal trying, with pathetic lack of theatrical skill, to impersonate professional guides or even railroad officials. They follow us back into the main terminal and up the stairs to the tourist office all the while barking and braying unintelligible verbiage, some metamorphosed blend of Hindi and English. Or maybe it's English spoken rapidly with Hindi intonations and no accented syllables. I cannot tell.

I don't even know for sure what they want. I suppose they are trying to sell us bogus tickets as they scribble numbers on forms and stuff them in our faces. Every so often, I recognize one repeated phrase. It sounds like "City Palace," which I assume to be the name of a hotel that would pay them kickbacks. To a sitcom audience, all this drama and confusion might appear hilarious, but to us conscripted improvisationalists, it is a nightmare.

I watch our luggage while Dick scurries from one office window to the next with no one agreeing to help. Part of the problem seems to be that it is now closing time. People are shutting windows, tallying books, turning off lights, going away. One man just ignores me, sitting inside his window a few inches from my face filling out paperwork even as I plead with him almost in tears. "We've missed our train. We're told we have to reserve seats two days in advance. We can't stay in Mumbai two more days. Won't you help us?" The man does not look up. He just keeps counting his bills.

This is one of the most helpless feelings I have ever experienced, second only to dangling from a rope down into a huge crevasse I once fell in while mountain climbing. Our itinerary is not so tight that we could not spare more time in Bombay. But we have no hotel reservations, and while we are not averse to camping out, the already over-camped streets of Bombay are not a pleasant prospect to consider. In fact, I feel desperate to get away from this city and the assault that its appalling living conditions make upon my conscience. People should not have to live this way while on the other side of the world so many Americans bask in tidiness and comfort.

Dick comes back, still followed by the skinny tout in the brown suit. But now the tout's verbiage is at least recognizable to me. He is yelling "City Palace City Palace City Palace," over and over as though it were a litany for his prayer beads.

"I got our ticket half refunded," Dick calls above the din of the touts' voices. "But they said we have to come back early in the morning when they first open up and get a new reservation. They think we can get it for tomorrow evening if we come early."

I breathe a sigh of partial relief. Half or maybe only a third of our problem is solved. But we still have to find a hotel, and that is surely what the tout is yelling about. Dick looks like a limp rag. He points to a reference in the guidebook called the *Railway Hotel.* "Can you phone this hotel? It's only a few blocks from here," he mumbles. As I take the book from him, Dick plops down on the edge of the big suitcase. I wonder if he's sick. The tout is still badgering him. The guy's strategy must be to break us down, collapse our nervous systems, so that we will have no spines left to do anything but follow him to whatever expensive scam he has in mind.

I agree to the task without much conviction. Surely it is my turn to do something more useful than standing around watching luggage. I take the book down to the main station where I had seen an STD stall. The tout heels behind. Besides the tout yelling at me, it is very noisy in the terminal with the crowds milling about and the public address system announcing trains. My programmable hearing aids are not up to the challenge. When I talk into the phone I can hear a male voice speaking on the other end of the line, but cannot understand a word he says. Then I remember Dick had said the hotel is only a few blocks away, so I yell into the receiver, "We'll come there and talk to you in person," and hang up. The tout follows us out onto the street still shouting, "City Palace, City Palace," very close to Dick's face. Dragging the heavy suitcase, Dick calls to me, "Ask someone the way to the Railway Hotel."

Ask someone? Who? I look around but find no one I consider to be a candidate for the job of information specialist. We have come into a sort of alleyway alongside of the railway station. Most of the people around here have practically no meat on their bones. Many of them are crouched beside little waist-high huts made of blackened tin and cardboard. I walk up to an elderly man wearing a long white robe who stands on a corner conversing with two women in crumpled saris. "Excuse me please," I say in as credible Hindi as I can muster. "Where is the Railway Hotel?" They stare at me in consternation for a moment, and then start shouting to one another in rapid Hindi. Perhaps they have misunderstood me and are arguing about what I meant.

Dick must be pretty incoherent because, as we continue on down the alleyway, he keeps pleading with me to ask someone for directions to the Railway Hotel. Had he not observed the results of my previous efforts? To be cooperative, I try again. At the corner a skeletal young man crouches over a fire. By the glow of the flames, I can see two scrawny razorback pigs rummaging through a pool of oily sewage near by. I tap the skeleton's arm and say, this time in slow, precise English. "Where is the Railway Hotel?" To my shock, a pair of eyes light up in his skull with an expression of evil glee that assures me this is an aspiring wannabe tout, certain that his golden opportunity has finally arrived. He jumps up and motions for Dick to follow him. "Come," he says, trying to grab the suitcase away from Dick.

Dick turns and starts to let go of the suitcase but I warn him in no uncertain terms. "No! It's another tout! Go that way!" I point him back onto his original course. Now we have two touts following us. Yelping in what must be Hindi at the tops of their lungs, they create a deafening roar that rattles my hearing aids. Then suddenly, to my immense relief, Dick points across the street and says, "Look! The sign! It says, "Railway Hotel."

Sure enough, on the opposite corner is a pleasant latticed window with a soft yellow lamp glowing within.

Inside, two hotel clerks with clean clothes on their sturdy frames deliver warm greetings and take our luggage. The touts follow us in, still babbling, but now they are focusing on the hotel staff instead of us. Although I don't literally understand a word, their message is clear. They are demanding payment from the Railway Hotel for delivering us to their door step. But Dick tells the desk clerk, "These guys have been hassling us unmercifully." Whereupon the hotel clerks bounce both scammers back outside. All is quiet now. My hearing aids have stopped rattling, but now I remember the sitcom audience I had imagined earlier. I can hear some of them cheering the demise of our tormentors. Others, however, feel sorry for the touts and sigh in sympathy for a pair of hungry predators who have worked so hard for a dinner that got away.

A porter ushers us into a clean room with its own white tiled bathroom. There is cold running water, a large bucket, and a small pitcher along side a drain in the floor. There is a squat style toilet consisting of a hole in the floor with foot platforms on either side. I deposit my long overdue contribution into the hole and flush it down by pouring cold water from the pitcher. After only one night in Bangkok and one in Bombay I have figured out how to clean my bottom by using the pitcher to dip cold water out of the bucket and pour it over my hand, how to take an adequate shower by spilling water over myself and onto the floor. The routine is becoming almost acceptable, so long as there is soap. The hotel has not provided soap, but I keep a small bar handy in my pack. I am learning to control my mind, teaching it never to think of our bath tub at home with its ever ready and ample supply of hot water.

I emerge from the bathroom wearing my night shirt to find Dick sitting on the bed in his under-shorts and staring at the guidebook. By that I don't mean he is propped up on fluffy pillows with clean sheets. This is a typical Asian style hotel. The mattress is a cotton stuffed muslin pad one and a half inches thick, quite firm. His pillow is a two inch pad of the same material. There are no sheets or pillow cases.

I pull our light silk sleeping bag liner out of its pouch and spread it on the bed. Dick lifts the book from his lap and stuffs his feet into the sack. "Since we have an extra day to kill in Bombay, we should take a boat ride over to Elephanta Island," he says. "The guidebook says it's Bombay's premier tourist attraction. There is an ancient Hindu temple carved into the hillside." He reads aloud, "Little is known about their origins, but they are thought to have been created between AD four-fifty and seven-fifty. It says there are some great carvings of Shiva and stories from Hindu mythology." I can see it coming. Dick's mind is already cataloging information. He'll soon be as expert on Hindu mythology as he already is on many other subjects. To our friends, I jokingly call him my walking encyclopedia.

"That sounds amazing! We really must see that!" Maybe Shiva screwed up our watches, so we would have a chance to visit him. I slide into the sheet sack beside Dick and squeeze his hand to show a bit of enthusiasm.

Dick inserts one of our *Bike for Global Democracy* brochures as a bookmark and sets the guidebook on the stand. He might as well use our brochures for something. Naïvely we had thought that, because India had been a British colony, there would be people who read English in almost every town. However, at Bentley's Guest House, the manager told us very few people speak English in the countryside between Agra and Bombay where we'll be cycling. So, we won't be distributing many English brochures there. In fact, he said many people there hate the British so much they refuse these days to allow their children to study English in school. Besides, there has been a recent revival of concern about the preservation of Hindi culture.

While reaching for the switch, my eyes follow the path of electric wiring along the center of the wall to a bare, exposed electric bulb, the room's only light source. I recall that we had once bought a house from a Turkish immigrant family in Seattle. We were amused that they had installed the wiring on the outside of the walls rather than hidden behind the sheetrock. Yet, I have noticed that in India exposed wiring appears to be more the norm than the exception. I knock on the wall a couple times. "I guess the walls here are too solid. Maybe there's no way to hide the wiring."

"More likely it costs too much to hide the wiring," says Dick.

I turn off the light and stare for a moment into total darkness. The room has no windows. I wonder how I will find the bathroom when I wake up in the middle of the night and have to use the toilet. I imagine wading into the bathroom with little pools of water hidden about like land mines. "It's pretty tough here in India. Are you sure we're up to this?"

Dick chuckles softly, then reaches around and cuddles up close to comfort me. "We'll likely survive. We've done all right so far."

"Those touts are pretty awful. How can they torment people like that?" I still feel shaken by our recent nightmarish escape from Victoria Station.

Dick says, "It's a protection racket. They figure we'll pay up to get them off our backs."

I think about this. Dick is right, but on the other hand, the existence of touts is just another natural consequence of massive poverty and unemployment. Touts are poorly educated men but energetic and resourceful. Maybe they have mouths to feed at home, if they have homes. They strive pathetically to imitate professional guides and make deals with hotels in hopes of squeezing a little spare money out of presumably wealthy tourists. Still it isn't easy to feel sorry for someone who is trying to rip us off. "We didn't pay them any money," I muse. But I'm not sure whether to feel smug or guilty.

"No, we didn't," agrees Dick with unequivocal satisfaction. "As I said, we've done all right so far."

"It could get pretty tiring, hassling with these characters all the time." Even more than hating them for making our lives miserable, I resent the touts for making me struggle with so many ambivalent feelings.

"It won't be like this in the countryside where we'll be bicycling. There won't be any touts," Dick assures me.

"Yes, I suppose it will be different when we're in the villages." I give his hand a reassuring squeeze. But I wonder how we will promote global democracy where no one speaks English. If only we had translated our brochures into Hindi. The purpose of our trip is to popularize the idea of a global parliament. How will we do that if we can't speak the language? The guidebook provides a few necessary Hindi phrases to help find food and lodging, but we had hoped to communicate at a deeper level.

CHAPTER 3

The Punjab Mail

Ten people are packed into this berth which has been reserved for only six. Most of our luggage, including the big suitcase containing an entire disassembled tandem bicycle, is stuffed under the seat. My feet are perched on its outer edge, which protrudes into the narrow floor space between our seat and the one across from us. My small pack is performing one of its usual collateral duties as lumbar support for my back. I feel people giving us disapproving looks for being obnoxious foreigners with an inordinate amount of luggage, but maybe I'm only projecting. No one has complained. At least none of the Hindi around me has been babbled in grumbling or complaining tones. In fact, everyone but me seems to be having a reasonably good time.

Four people sit in the seat opposite us. Their bags of heavy embroidered cloth and simple burlap are stuffed in around them. An older woman, clearly of grandmotherly status, sits crossed legged yoga style directly in front of me. There is no space for her feet except underneath her. I cannot judge this woman's age, but there is an air of maturity about her which makes me, at age sixty-four, feel like a foolish child in her presence. Draped in a large black sari with white lace trim, she reminds me of the great raven from Native

American folk art. I wonder what sort of weird creature I resemble to those intelligent dark eyes staring unabashedly at my face. It feels as though her gaze could penetrate my skull to the inner workings of my brain. At first this is unsettling, but the more I think about it, the more comforting it seems. Mind reading would remove some of the profound language and cultural barriers that separate me from this other human being with whom I must share a small space for the night. Without it, we might just as well be watching one another through the bars of a zoo cage, observing with curiosity but never really getting acquainted.

The cage image is a good metaphor for this sleeper car on the Punjab Mail. Except for the padded seats, everything is gray-green metal. Small greasy windows opened to the warm evening breeze, are partially crisscrossed with gray-green bars. A gray metal ladder leads up to the overhead shelf. The floor is covered with black rubber matting, excellent material for catching any unwanted crumbs or droppings from the cage's inhabitants. A little boy, apparently the grandson of the raven woman, has deposited himself on the shelf. His large black eyes gaze anxiously at me in the manner of a squirrel looking down from a tree, alert and ready to dart away in case I should move too quickly or do anything unexpected.

A vendor, perhaps in his late teens, wends his way through the crowd. "Chai? . . . Chai? . . . Chai?" He calls in a high pitched chant. I remember that I still have a paper napkin with some bananas and boiled eggs in my pack, left-overs from breakfast at the Railway Hotel. I nudge Dick's arm and say, "Let's have some tea." Chai, boiled eggs, and bananas will make a sufficient dinner for me. In fact, I'm sure that, if there were nothing in the world but boiled eggs, bananas, and tea, I would survive in good health.

The vendor pours the chai from a spigot on the side of a stainless steel jug into tiny plastic glasses. It is thick milky syrup, in Seattle terms, a very short chai latte. This important drink is used in India at various times of the day, mostly late morning and afternoon, to pep oneself up or to offer friends as a gesture of hospitality. Everyone seems to give us approving glances at our choice of drinks, but I feel many pairs of eyes focused on me in wonder and disbelief when I haul out the boiled eggs and bananas. While eating I collect the peelings, shells, plastic glasses in the napkin and make a little bundle of garbage on my lap. The raven woman's eyes still penetrate my brain as I glance around the berth in search of a waste basket. She lifts her skinny talons and motions toward the open window. Her communication is clear and emphatic. This woman, clearly my superior in status here, is ordering me in no uncertain terms to do something that is not only unlawful in my home state but also against the important seventh principle of my Unitarian religion. She is ordering me to litter.

I shake my head. What else can I do? How can I explain to this stranger who does not understand my language, that I would sooner steal or fornicate in public than litter.

The raven woman's eyes continue to penetrate my skull and the talons to motion out the window.

I shake my head again.

The raven woman ruffles her feathers in desperation as if trying to communicate with a moron. Next she issues an order in rapid Hindi to the little boy perched on the shelf above. He scurries down, seizes the plastic bag from my lap, and tosses it out the window. So much for the garbage. By now, everyone is staring at this white headed moron old lady.

Embarrassed, I remove a book from my pack and pretend to read.

My watch says it's nine o'clock PM in India although my brain has no idea what time it really is, having long since lost touch with its Seattle circadian rhythms and not yet caught up with Indian time. We had arisen before dawn this morning so we could arrive at the station in time to reserve our seats on the evening train. On the way, we had stepped around and sometimes over dozens of children sleeping on the dusty sidewalks. The station had not yet opened when we arrived and there was a long line in front. After awhile the door had opened slightly, just enough for one person at a time to squeeze through. Immediately people began pushing and shoving one another aside in competition to get through the door.

Despite the brutal mayhem, we managed to get inside the station unharmed and were relieved to find that we could wait peacefully in front of the tourist ticket window without any harassment from touts. After we got our tickets, we returned to the Railway Hotel for a delicious breakfast buffet included in the room fee. While feasting on curried rice and mangos, I furtively stuffed the boiled eggs and bananas into my bag in case they might come in handy later in the day.

We spent most of the day visiting Elephanta Island caves, a soul expanding adventure. My art education class back in college, focused as it had been on western civilization, had never mentioned such sophisticated and representational carvings going as far back as the seventh century AD. Many of the works had been damaged later when invading Portuguese had used them for target practice. But the most important piece was still intact. That was a graceful three faced representation of Shiva, father of the gods, shown as creator, preserver and destroyer. I meditated upon this sophisticated theological concept during another frightening taxi ride back to Victoria Station.

Now on the crowded train, my mind's eye still views the smooth stone face of Shiva, with its softly curved eye lids. Out there in the void beyond my half closed eyes an ocean of warm night air pours through the open window swimming with variable smells of metallic smoke, sweet cardamom spice, open sewers. Unsettling the current of smell is another onslaught of sound, the drone of Hindi conversation, the chanting of food vendors working the crowd, the train whistling through towns, other trains rumbling by on the opposite track. I can feel myself drifting off from the sheer exhaustion of this sensual assault as part of my mind wonders on whose lap my head will fall. This was supposed to be a sleeper train. I had thought that meant there would be room to lie down.

Suddenly I feel tugging at my arm. I open my eyes to see a man gesturing toward another seat across the aisle. Dick says, "Mona, you have to sit over there while we rearrange the berths for sleeping." But I barely have time to get up, stumble across the aisle and sit down again before the entire scene has been completely transformed. People shuffle about changing positions. The backs of seats become middle bunks; luggage comes down from shelves to be stuffed under seats. Magically, instead of two seats in our section, there are now six bunks.

"This is your bed, Mona," explains Dick, motioning for me to claim the entire seat upon which four of us had previously been seated. It makes a nice big bottom bunk on which I proceed to stretch out in full view of everyone. But no one is staring at me now. Everyone is busy settling themselves into their own sleeping spaces, pulling blankets over themselves, stuffing pillows under their heads, tucking in their kids. I take off my shoes, put my glasses into one of them and store them along the wall at the end of my bunk. I lay my towel over the top of my back pack which now assumes another one of its collateral duties as my pillow for the night. Dick places our sleeping bag liner over me for cover before climbing up to take his place on the middle bunk. The breeze rushing through the open window is cooler now, so I pull the cover around my head and drift off into the ocean of smell and sound on the gentle rocking of the train.

Next my subconscious mind is waking me up to say my bladder is full. It has been a couple of decades since I could sleep through the night without getting up to take a leak. I put on my glasses, crawl to the end of my bunk and peer around the corner in the direction of the toilet only to find the floor of the aisle completely stuffed with male bodies, most of them in military uniform. There would be no way to get through to the bathroom without stepping on a number of them. I look at my watch. It's only two o'clock. Maybe my bladder will tolerate a bit more pressure before I really need to go. I put my glasses back in the shoe and lie down again wedging my back against the wall to give the bladder more support. I am drifting off again.

It is four o'clock when I wake up next, but this time there is no denying the bladder. I take my glasses out of my shoe and put them on. I also put on my shoes. Then I peer around the corner again, carefully examining the floor for every possible foot space. I step gingerly into the aisle and wend my way to the end of the car, feeling the crush of flesh and bone under foot several times, each time whispering profuse apologies. Fortunately no one seems to wake up. At the end of the car, I see that the alcove between the cars is also covered with bodies. Three large trunks are stacked chest high in front of the bathroom door. A young man in military uniform dozes on top of the trunks. To avoid stepping on any-more bodies, I climb up over the trunks and squeeze myself be-tween them and the door.

The gray-green metal toilet stall is about the size of an old fashioned U.S. telephone booth. It has a hole in the floor be-tween metal foot-treads smeared with soggy excrement. Beside that are a tiny metal wash basin, and a low faucet. There is no bucket or pitcher. By the dim light shining through the hole, I can see the ties of the railroad tracks passing underneath. The floor is flooded with an inch of water. In doing my business, I take great care to make sure that the ends of my pants legs don't touch the floor.

* * * * *

When I awaken again there is a touch of gray light coming through the window. I look out and see a pink line along the edge of a level horizon. Thirsty misshapen trees speckle the brown landscape. We pass a village of huts made of blackened concrete, corrugated tin, and burlap. Piles of rubbish, plastic bags, news-paper, and tin cans litter the yards. We cross a sluggish, shallow river covered with scum and debris. It gives off a murky sheen in the growing light.

As I lay watching the landscape drift by outside, sounds re-awaken from within the train. Conversations resume. People start milling about in the aisles, pulling down luggage, rearranging bunks. Dick climbs down from his bunk, and we lower it to replace the back of our seat again. A boy comes through selling chai. I reach in my pocket for some rupees and call out to him, "Chai, please."

The train stops in a station. People stand in family group-ings on the platform outside bowing and greeting, taking leave of one another. A festive atmosphere surrounds the stalls outside selling magazines, handkerchiefs, and steaming pots of food. Dick spots a banana vendor and darts for the exit. I see him through the window pointing and haggling over the price. He comes back with a little bunch of bananas and two small newspaper cones full of rice and nuts, sweetly spiced.

While we eat, a white-bearded man, withered with age, passes through the train proffering a silver bowl, obviously meant for donations. The bright red spot on his forehead, the cheeks and arms heavily painted with white stripes suggest that he must be a monk or holy man. A garland of flowers and several strands of orange beads hang over his bare chest, and a dusty, faded orange cloth is tied around the lower half of his body. Some passengers drop coins in his bowl. I reach in my pocket and find a five rupee coin for him.

After breakfast, I feel my internal organs calling again, so I head for the toilet stall. The aisle is still crowded, but at least there isn't anyone lying in it. However, a queue of several people waits for the toilet. The man standing in front of me in line greets me with a bow holding his palms in front of his face and says, "Namaste." I return his gesture with a friendly smile. When his turn comes, the man steps aside and motions for me to go ahead of him. "No, it's your turn," I object.

"No, you go," he insists. "You are our guest. Guest is god."

Overwhelmed with embarrassment, I say, "Thank you, sir. Thank you very much." It had not occurred to me that anyone on this train would consider me a guest. To me, I am another passenger just like them. But, on the other hand, I am a stranger, and this man is very much at home here.

The next stop is a larger town. Lots of people get off, and the train is not so crowded. This town seems a little more prosperous. Some of the buildings, including the station house, are made of red brick. There is not as much trash on the ground. Several more people get off. A little boy crawls by in the aisle reaching under our seat, sweeping food crumbs and garbage down to the next booth. Then he raises his palms and gazes up with pleading eyes. Everyone ignores him. Soon another boy crawls down the aisle from the opposite direction and sweeps the same garbage back into our booth. Then he begs from the people in the other booth. Dick looks at me, shrugs, and smiles sadly. It's as if we are watching a parade or procession, for along comes another boy beating a drum. Two little girls in bright pink saris bounce along behind in an artless dance. I pay the dancers each five rupees.

At the next station, the raven woman gets off along with a large entourage of her relatives. A young family gets on and takes their seats. Draped in a lemon yellow sari, the mother sits directly across from me, her sweet oval face looking thoughtfully out the window. There are two children. The son, who seems to be about five years old, sits between his parents gazing at me in rapt wonder as if I am a creature from outer space. The daughter, who seems to be about eleven, takes little notice of us. She spends a lot of time climbing up and down from the overhead shelf. Soon she leaves the train car and comes back later with another little girl who climbs up and down with her. They seem to be using the ladder and upper berth as a jungle gym. The parents accept this graciously as the normal, harmless children's behavior that it is. Indian parents seem naturally endowed with good parenting skills. It never occurs to them, as it does to so many U.S. parents, to needlessly harass and torment their children.

Neat and bespectacled in clean brown slacks, precisely creased, sits the father directly across from Dick. They are already getting acquainted. "You are from what country?" The man speaks slowly punching out each syllable separately like spots of color on a paint-by-number board. I reach in my pack for my hearing aids. Finally I can hope to benefit from them.

"America," says Dick.

"Canada?"

"USA."

"America! You come from America!" he exclaims in an astonished tone. "What is your profession?"

"I am a retired mathematician."

"A mathematician? You were a professor?"

"Well yes, a long time ago, but I worked twenty years for the Boeing Company as a mathematician and engineer."

"I am engineer also. I am transportation engineer for India Railways."

"That's wonderful!" Dick says. "You have a great rail system in India." I am not certain whether by engineer the man means that he drives trains or what, but I can sense Dick's excitement at the mention of trains. He loves them and advocates for rail transit improvements back home.

"Yes," the man agrees. "India Railways is the world's largest employer. We have over a million and a half employees. We have nearly seventy thousand kilometers of track. You can see much of our country by train."

"Yes, it's great! We're having a wonderful time on the train! Best transportation system in the world!" agrees Dick.

"But when we get to Agra, we will bicycle back to Mumbai," I say.

"Bicycle?" He pantomimes pedaling with his feet and holding handle bars with his fists as if to make sure he heard the right word.

The man's head swivels in my direction as it begins to wobble back and forth in confusion and disbelief. Whereupon Dick launches into another of his favorite topics, magnifying the man's bewilderment with the information that our bicycle built for two has been disassembled and packed into our suitcase.

The man waves his hand at the suitcase under my feet. "How will you carry all that luggage?"

"When we are bicycling, the suitcase becomes a trailer which we pull behind us," says Dick.

The man's head wobbles like a whirl-i-gig on a stick, as Dick expounds upon the wonders of Oregon bicycle design technology.

Meanwhile I focus on the man's son who is still staring at me. I decide to test his English. "What is your name?" I ask. At first he doesn't seem to know I'm talking to him, He turns to see whether I'm really looking at someone else. I get this reaction often because I have a visual impairment called exotropia. My eyes are forty degrees misaligned.

"What is your name?" echoes the mother, encouraging her son to answer.

He gives me a startled smile as if amazed that I would speak to him. "My name is Sharma."

"Sharma is learning English in Kindergarten," the mother declares with pride. "He knows lots of songs."

Thus cued, little Sharma begins to sing, "Baa baa black sheep have you any wool . . ."

"Yes, sir, yes sir three bags full," I join in. Without missing a beat, Sharma gapes at me in shock, as if he thinks no one outside his school room would know this song.

When that song is finished, Sharma begins another, "Jingle

bells, jingle bells, jingle all the way," we sing together. Thanks to
Sharma, I am finally having as much fun as everyone else on the
Punjab Mail. I cannot believe the month of December has arrived, jingle bell season, time for "a one horse open sleigh." Outside the sun shines high in the sky as we pass fields of young
wheat and paddies of rice. A warm wind blows across my face.
I'm beginning to share Dick's appreciation for the Indian transportation system. Back home millions of holiday travelers sit alone
in motorized wheel cages, barreling down icy freeways. Here we
socialize in a summer-like party atmosphere. Best of all, I've met
someone who speaks my language. We even know the same songs.

* * * *

The Punjab Mail arrives in Agra at six thirty-five PM, about two
hours later than we had told Gaurau Singh to expect us. Using a large
brown envelope, I have improvised a sign with his name on it. I hope
we can find him. Recalling our hectic experience of searching for last
minute shelter a couple of nights ago in Bombay, I am not eager for a
repeat performance.

No one takes much notice of my sign, no one except for two inevitable touts who sneer at it while attaching themselves to either side of us
like bodyguards. We completely ignore them, however, and head straight
for the passenger waiting room where touts are not allowed. Just before
entering, I turn to them and, just for fun, shout, "Shoo!"

One of them gives me a startled look and says, "Shoo!' With that,
they vanish as though I had said the magic word.

After we set our luggage down in the waiting room, Dick turns to
me and says, "Will you find a phone and try to call Mr. Singh?"

I feel dubious about agreeing to do this but want to prove that
perhaps I am good for something. So I venture out into the station and
walk all the way to the opposite end, straining for the slightest trace of
a phone. Finally I spot a booth under a large sign that reads, "Handicap
Assistance." I walk up to the booth and explain to the man inside that
I have a visual impairment and that I need to make a phone call.

Gesturing, the man directs me to go out of the station building
onto the main street. "Turn left, go one block and turn left again."
Shortly thereafter, he assures me, I will find an STD stall on the right
side of the street. At least that's what I think he says.

In order to reach the exit, I have to walk all the way back past Dick and the passenger waiting room. By this time I have chickened out of the errand. It is dark outside. I imagine that there will be lots of male strangers out there, many of them touts. So I relay the directions to Dick and prevail upon him to make the call himself while I stay in the waiting room watching the luggage.

Depressed by the exposed wiring and grimy walls of the waiting room, I escape into a novel, *The Death of Vishnu*, about life in Bombay.

Half an hour later, Dick comes panting back. "I've reached Mr. Singh," he says. "He'll be here shortly."

After a couple more chapters, a young man with an air of gentle confidence and nicely padded bones comes in. "I am Gaurau Singh, and you must be Mona Lee. I am honored to meet you," he says. This is clearly not a tout.

We show Gaurau the Servas list with the phone number for Sant Doss Srivastava which actually had turned out to be his own phone number.

Gaurau looks at the number and smiles. "All the phone numbers in Agra have changed since this list was made," he says. "But I think I know what the correct number should be." He reaches in his breast pocket and pulls out a cell phone, fingers the keys, and babbles cheerfully into it. Then he puts the phone back in his pocket and lays out the plan. "We take you to nice reasonably priced hotel tonight. Tomorrow my religious leader will guide you on tour of Agra's temples and the Taj Mahal. Afterwards, we go to Mr. Srivastava. He is eager to meet you."

CHAPTER 4

What is a God?

Sharing the road on our first day of biking in India.

It's only our first day of biking in India, but Dick boldly usurps the left edge of the black top and lets two big trucks roar around us. At scary times like this, I wish Dick would drop down onto the rock studded shoulder out of the fray, but he says that would be hard on our tires. Another truck waits behind honking indignantly in demand of room to pass between us and a loping camel cart whose driver gapes sideways at us in abject wonder. After all, in this corner of the world an old white couple on a bike is positively bizarre in contrast with the mundane appearance of a camel driver sitting on a mountain of stuffed burlap bags, his white turban bobbing up and down.

Paparazzi of six or more young males on identical black bicycles draft in the wind-wake behind. We don't know who they are or where they came from. They just materialize from no where. And they follow. Relentlessly. Surely they won't harm us. They are just curious. We are a carnival attraction, the circus wagon come to town. That's why people walk along the dusty shoulder of the road grinning and pointing at us. That's why so many heads hang out of bus windows. A jitney stops ahead and lets all its passengers out just to watch us pass as if we were a parade float.

Will we ever come to the Sundaram Restaurant, or was it the Sandoorum Restaurant, where our Servas host, Sant Doss Srivastava, said to meet him? We can see chai wallas and food stalls along the way, and we pass a couple of what look like outdoor restaurants, but the names on their signs bare no resemblance to the sound Sant Doss had shouted back as his motorcycle charged on ahead.

We have already crossed five intersections, whereas Sant Doss had said the restaurant would be on the left hand side just past the third intersection. "Maybe we've missed it somehow," I call to Dick up front. But I wish I hadn't because that prompts him to stop and look at the map.

As if by magic they appear from all directions, a human fortress closing in around us. There is scarcely room to breath. The closest ones are just inches away. Perhaps fifty to a hundred men of every size and age, mostly wearing loose slacks and cotton shirts. This is an exclusively male crowd. One lonely woman in a dusty sari stalks by carrying a load of firewood on her head. She does not stop, but leers at us as she walks around the men and onto the hot pavement in her bare feet.

Dick smiles for the camera surrounded by curious residents.

Many of the men are also barefoot, but some wear flip-flops or sandals. Dozens of dusty toes confront us casually as if to affirm the superfluity of our cleated bicycling shoes and other mysterious paraphernalia, the glossy helmets, my loud pink nylon windbreaker, the four white plastic water bottles attached to the shiny blue frame of our bike. The mob stares in silence, dozens of dark eyes peering at our small front wheels, the long chain passing through an inexplicable array of gears and levers. Their gaze moves up to our wrinkled, pale faces and down to our suitcase trailer draped with its gray banner sporting a big logo of the earth superimposed over a bicycle wheel and the inscrutable English words, "Bike for Global Democracy."

This is our first day on the road bicycling, and I have had very little success in uttering carefully rehearsed phrases in a manner understandable to anyone. Sant Doss tried to teach me to give each syllable equal emphasis as there are no accented ones in Hindi. He said I must learn to say my R's correctly, but that sound thumps off my tongue somewhere between English "th" and a "d." "San-da-dam thes-tau-dant?" I ask, gesturing and gawking around in charade of searching. At first there is no reaction, but now heads turn toward one another and wobble back and forth. One young man opens a gap-toothed mouth and shouts something in Hindi. Everyone laughs. Someone responds with another Hindi phrase. Everyone laughs again. Shouts and laughter erupt like mini-geysers throughout the crowd.

"Sundarum Restaurant?" Dick bravely tries again.

The gap toothed man first wobbles his head, and then shakes it emphatically. "No." The message is clear. No one has ever heard of anything called by the dubious syllables we have tried to utter.

"Maybe we should go on. It's probably just a little farther now," I suggest.

"Unless we've passed it already," says Dick. "The sign may have been in Hindi."

"Wouldn't Sant Doss wait out in front for us? Let's go on a little farther, and if we don't find him, we'll turn around and come back." But I'm not sure whether we can move forward, trapped as we are in this pen of people.

As Dick pushes the bike forward, the crowd parts enough for us to squeeze through. I follow cautiously holding up the rear of the bike and watching to make sure the trailer wheels don't get caught on anything. As we move forward, the crowd follows, closing in around us. We aren't making much headway . . . They continue to quip and chortle, as if making fun of a two-headed man in a side show.

"We might as well remount," suggests Dick.

As we start to mount up, the people in front of us move aside. A pleasant looking young man walks toward us. "Would you like some tea?" he asks in clear, precise English. He motions toward the side of the road where, under a large tree, stands a typical stall made of rough cut poles. The roof is a piece of tin tied with bailing twine to the top of the poles. Behind the counter stands another young man over a bubbling cauldron of milky chai. He places two glasses on the counter, and then holds aloft a large strainer through which he pours a long stream of chai syrup into the glasses.

Even though I know Sant Doss is probably already waiting for us at the Sundaram, or whatever it's called, wherever it is, I cannot pass this up. I'm hungry and exhausted. A cup of chai would hold me over nicely until we do find Sant Doss and the elusive restaurant.

"Oh, yes, thank you," I agree without hesitation.

"Come sit in our shop." The first young man gestures invitingly toward a bench under the roof.

I glance around at the crowd. "What would we do with the bicycle?"

"My friend will make sure no one harms your cycle while you have tea."

Dick and I sit down cautiously on the bench. The young man pulls up a wooden box for a stool and sits down in front of us. "This is my home. You are welcome here," he says glancing around at the humble interior. For floor, there is nothing but dirt and rock. The underside of the tin roof is blackened with soot.

"Thank you very much," I say.

"You are from what country?" He proceeds with the inevitable conversation starter.

"USA."

"USA? What brings you here?"

"We are bicycling for peace," says Dick.

"We are promoting the idea of a global parliament elected by the peoples of the world," I say. "We will bicycle to Bombay and attend the World Social Forum." I reach in the breast pocket of my pink jacket and pull out a clear plastic envelope containing a newspaper clipping and show it to the young man. The entire article is visible through the plastic. There is a picture of me and Dick on the bike dressed in our bicycle helmets, khaki pants, and colorful bicycle jerseys. The article is in Hindi, so I cannot read it myself but Sant Doss has translated for us. It says we are followers of Gandhi on a mission to promote world peace. It explains that we are bicycling because that is an environmentally friendly way to travel. Besides, we want to see the real India and connect with the people. It goes on to say that our destination is Mumbai where we will attend the World Social Forum and help to organize a coalition to promote the idea of a democratically elected global parliament.

The young man takes the article and holds it in his open palms, like a prayer book, his lips moving as he reads silently. Then he looks at us with new admiration. "Thank you for what you do," he says and hands me back the article.

By this time, I have finished my tea. I hand him the glass. "How much for the tea? How many rupees?"

He shakes his head. "No charge. You are guest. Guest is god."

Guest is god. I have heard that before. It was just a few days ago on the train. I think of what our friend Timothy had said over three dollar lattes in a trendy Seattle coffee shop. "Remember you are a wallet, not a person." He must have visited a different India than this.

Guest is god. I have been trying to figure out what this word god means in India. There are so many gods. It must be a word like love, a word with many meanings. I recall the day before yesterday in Agra with Gaurau and Senjeev. I had spent most of the time trying to understand Hindu theology, but I had felt blown through the experience like Dorothy on a Kansas tornado.

* * * * *

Our first night in Agra, I had walked with Gaurau out of the railway station to where a driver waited with a miniscule black car. I looked dubiously at the car, then at our enormous pile of luggage. Gaurau and the driver, obviously assisted by a host of invisible attendant gods, managed to stuff everything inside. My duffle bag and Dick's pack were bulging out of the car's mini-trunk when Gaurau slammed the door aggressively to force them the rest of the way in. To my amazement, the door clicked shut. Then he wedged the big suitcase containing the disassembled bike in between the seats. Finally we squeezed ourselves into the seats on either side of the suitcase.

The little bumper car raced through darkened streets alive with headlights darting about in all directions. It was like a battle scene from *Star Wars* and, speaking of gods, the Force must have been with us. Lights sped toward us as we likewise charged them in a game of chicken. Then suddenly, a split second before inevitable collision, they would dart away. But the deafening background music for this movie was a cacophony of honking, shrieking, and trumpeting. Eventually we pulled into a narrow dark street lined with vendor stalls and flaming food braziers. The car doors were flung mysteriously open from the outside and we poured into the street jumping and darting around to avoid being hit by the rapid rocket-fire of headlights.

Gaurau led us down a dark passage way into a dingy courtyard. The dubious light shining through an open doorway revealed a motley array of walls, gates and fences arranged haphazardly at various angles. We passed through the lit doorway into a small room with silk cushioned couches arranged along the walls. Barely visible in the light were white stucco walls hung with paintings of one dimensional floral patterns, each signed in two inch letters by an amateur artist named Etka. A broad low coffee table occupied most of the floor space between the couches. The source of the dim light proved to be a single bulb protruding from the wall at about standing eye level.

A young gentleman, positively stout by Indian standards, sat cross-legged yoga style on a silky overstuffed couch. He wore a bright red shirt and there was a big crimson spot painted on his forehead. Small intense eyes captured the light, giving them a mysterious gleam, brighter than anything else in the room. No temple idol could have made a better god. A long train of authoritative syllables, vaguely recognizable as English, tumbled out of the god's mouth. It was difficult to make much sense of what he said, other than that we were cordially welcomed and invited to sit down.

I reached up and turned my programmable hearing aids to a higher volume, whereupon I learned that this was Senjeev, a Hindu priest. Tonight we would be taken to a nice, reasonably priced hotel. In the morning Senjeev would give us a tour of Agra including the Taj Mahal. "Senjeev will guide you. His English is better, and he knows much Hindu culture," Gaurau explained. Dick and I looked at one another and smiled. We both found Gaurau's English far more decipherable than Senjeev's, no matter what the differential might be in theological status or years of schooling. As it turned out, next day Dick lucked out and got Gaurau for his guide. It was I, the one with the diagnosed hearing impairment, who was assigned to Senjeev. Senjeev clung to my arm and spoke earnestly though unintelligibly into my ear for the entire afternoon.

Something had told me this would be an occasion to wear the

one and only excuse for a dress I had brought with me on the trip. It was a full length black skirt of T-shirt material, actually designed to be worn with a T-shirt. My maroon T-shirt decorated with a golden tree pattern hung down over my waist line. Shenjeev wore dark pants and a beautiful red tartan shirt that nicely matched the red spot on his forehead. I was eager to see the photos Dick snapped of me and Senjeev parading through dusty narrow market streets buzzed by rickshaws and jostled by crowds. Because of the combination of Senjeev's accent, my hearing impairment, and persistent background noise from crowds and traffic, I cannot say that I picked up many actual facts about Hinduism, but even so I came away with an impression of spirituality in India.

At our first stop on the tour, Senjeev paraded us up the iron staircase of a dark factory built with a giant erecter set of steel girders bolted together, our footsteps gonging like kettle drums all the way up. I had no idea what we were doing there even after Senjeev finally explained, "This is gold and jewel market. My friend has new business. Opens tomorrow." I certainly hoped they did not think of us as potential customers. A pair of K-Mart earrings is as close as I have ever come to jewels.

At the top of the stairs was a hallway with a row of brilliantly lit

The author and her guide, Senjeev, pose in the streets of Agra.

vendor stalls as yet containing no merchandise. Made of mirrors
etched with leafy vines and floral patterns, their extravagant walls
stood in breathtaking contrast with the industrial poverty below.
Senjeev ushered us to an open doorway and asked us to take off our
shoes. We had no idea what would happen next.

Inside was a plain metallic office, but between the filing cabinet
and the wall was a miniature shrine no more that two feet tall. There
was a small white marble altar with two tiny pillars flanking a graceful ink drawing of Shiva and his wife Pavrati. The picture was draped
with a garland of marigolds. "Please sit, Madame," instructed Senjeev,
lowering himself gracefully into a yogic position. I knelt and bowed
low before the shrine, inhaling the florescent air before curling my knees
underneath my skirt. Throughout numerous meditation classes, my
stiff joints have stubbornly refused to contort themselves into the shape
of a lotus flower.

Senjeev lit several sticks of incense emitting a sweet pink cloud
into the floral air. Then he began to chant in a rich tenor. Every so
often Gaurau and several other gentlemen who had come in behind
us would reply with another chant they all knew by heart. Intermittently, Senjeev would place rose petals or little oil lamps on the altar.
After the quarter hour ceremony, Senjeev took my arm and helped
me up. Then he looked directly into my eyes and asked, "How do
you feel, Madame?"

"Wonderful!" I said, surprised to find that I was not even exag-
gerating, let alone lying. I assumed we had just participated in the
blessing of a new business, and the ardor of this simple ritual had
summoned a spiritual presence, perhaps a god, in the place.

My memory of the rest of that warm afternoon is more like a
whirl-wind or maybe a dream. We did a lot of charging about through
crowded market streets in a taxi. The driver seemed to be training
for a day job in formula one race cars, as he sped within millimeters
of pedestrians and auto rickshaws by the dozens without harming
anyone or anything. Maybe that was because on his dash board
there was a statue of Ganesh, the elephant faced god who removes
all obstacles.

The taxi would drop us off at the end of some narrow alley way,
and we would all pile out. Tugging at my arm, Senjeev would pull

me through the crowd as we darted here and there to avoid being run over by other aspiring Mario Andretti's. All the while, Senjeev emitted into my ear a choo-choo train of not quite recognizable syllables. At first, I tried asking him to repeat himself, but I soon gave up. No matter how many times he emitted the same verbiage, it made no more sense to me.

A block or more before we would reach a temple, Senjeev would indicate that it was time to remove our shoes. I recalled one of Joan's medical warnings. "Don't dare to take sandals to India. You must wear thick covered shoes at all times. What if you had a cut that got infected?" So there I was barefoot jumping about to avoid being hit by taxis and motorcycles while steering a zigzag course over sharp stones, aluminum cans, and sundry litter.

I lost count myself, but Dick says Senjeev and Gaurau took us to five temples. What seemed strange was the obscurity of these ancient places of worship. Unlike European cathedrals or old New England churches, these sacred sites were not set off at a distance to be admired as we approached. Buried as they were in food stands, fabric shops and pharmacy stalls, I never saw any of them until we were already inside. Prompted either by austerity concerns, lack of esthetic sensitivity, the total absence of zoning ordinances, or all of the above, the outer walls of these historic buildings performed double duty as the backs of sundry business establishments. Inside, ancient wall carvings and ornate columns were juxtaposed with exposed wiring, pipes, peeling green paint, and bare light bulbs. Often we waded barefoot on stone floors awash with puddles or streams.

The number of historic sites we visited that afternoon was insignificant in comparison with the huge pantheon of gods to which we were introduced. I'm sorry to say that I did not catch many of their names and have already forgotten most of the ones I heard. Let's see, there were Doji, Ganesh, and the Kali Ma. I draw a blank. Each temple featured a number of altars upon which were perched little god idols. Some were beautiful and exquisitely carved like the face of Shiva at Elephanta Island, but most were amorphous characters with barely recognizable features. Many were covered with gaudy paint. Gold was the most popular color, but there were also bright red gods, blue and green ones with scary or comical eyes and weird facial features painted on as in a child's crayon drawing. Some were barely more than chunks of rock adorned with the most exquisite gold crowns and draped in matching robes.

For every god, we performed a series of prescribed rituals, floating about with scores of other worshipers in a cloud of saccharine incense. It amazed me the way people did all this with pious fervor as intense as falling in love. But what amazed me more was the way I got into it myself. At Senjeev's suggestion, we knelt before every god, rang bells, purchased flowers, candies, and tiny oil lamps to lay upon their altars. Celebrants rewarded our piety by hanging garlands of flowers around our necks and painting big red spots on our foreheads. I soon felt festooned as a little god myself. At one point a celebrant gave me water to drink and, as it touched my lips, I recalled Joan's warnings about never drinking liquid of unknown origin. Even so, I took a cowardly sip.

As Senjeev led me by the arm out of each temple, he would turn to me and say, "How do you feel, Madame."

"Wonderful!" I would reply and not be lying.

Although we had promised Sant Doss that we would come to his house for lunch at two-thirty, it was nearly three o'clock when we finally reached the Taj Mahal, and I wasn't about to pass up that part of the tour. As a child I had seen it in a travel movie about the Seven Wonders of the World. I decided then that if I ever got to see the Taj in person, my lust for travel would be satiated. I would essentially have seen everything.

So there I was walking arm in arm with Senjeev beside a long pool of water in the direction of perfect symmetry. On either side were the first completely unlittered stretches of grass we had yet seen in India. The pristine whiteness of the monument rose like a snow covered peak against a blue cloudless sky, the frontal view enabling the visibility of all minarets, onion domes, and graceful pointed arches at once. In the exuberance of the moment, I wanted to repay the gods for bringing me here so I made the mistake of saying to Senjeev, "This building reminds me in a way of Mount Rainier, our big tourist attraction in Washington State. The Native American peoples worship that mountain as

Garau, Dick and Senjeev pose in front of the Taj Mahal.

the god, Tahoma. I hope someday you and Gaurau can come see
it with us."

Senjeev halted in his tracks and looked at me. "I would love
to come to America. But you would have to help me."

"How?"

"Write letter to your consulate. Say you want me to visit."

"I would be glad to!" I said. We were getting close enough to
see the marble facade with its detail-work reminiscent of scallops and floral patterns on pure white table linens. "It's so beautiful," I said, trying to change the subject.

I could hear Gaurau instructing Dick in fairly intelligible English. "Taj Mahal is most beautiful building in the world. It is monument to love. It was grave for young wife of Emperor Shah Jahan.
She died in childbirth back in the 16ᵗʰ Century. It took 70 years to
build this mausoleum."

As we strolled around the expansive white marble interior, I
thought about the woman buried there. Probably if she had lived to
be a chubby wrinkled granny with dozens of progeny, this woman
would be long forgotten. Was she a great beauty or just an ordinary

nice person? I wondered what this incredibly wealthy couple's relationship was like; whether the lives of ordinary poor people in the surrounding countryside were any better in those days than now; how many millions of other tourists have pondered these questions before?

The last stop on our tour was a parapet in back of the Taj overlooking the river. While I was snapping more photos, Senjeev looked at me again in earnest and said, "You help me come to America?"

"I could write a letter saying I want you to visit," I said, hoping he would not expect me to pay for his airline ticket.

Overhearing Senjeev's plea, Dick said, "It's very difficult to come to the United States. When my first wife died her sister from Thailand could not get a visa to come to the funeral."

Senjeev looked devastated. "Why not?"

"The family would have been required to pay thousands of dollars. We didn't have that kind of money."

"I want to teach yoga in America. I am good teacher," persisted Senjeev.

I smiled to myself, recalling the futility of poor Senjeev's efforts that afternoon to teach me the basics of Hinduism. His English would have to improve considerably or he would need bright young students with acute hearing. However, I left it up to Dick to shatter his dream. "They make it hard for people to come to America because they're afraid you will want to work there," Dick explained.

"Senjeev looked at me desperately. "Maybe tell them I am your son," he suggested.

I could feel my lips curling in an embarrassed smile. "No one would believe that," I said. But I regretted the remark for it hurt Senjeev. He fell silent and spoke very little in the taxi on the way home. I was silent too, pondering millions of promising young people like Senjeev constricted by arbitrary rules designed to limit their freedom. It hardly seemed fair that Senjeev could treat me to such a wonderful afternoon but that I could not return the favor.

It was well after dark by the time we finished the tour and dropped Senjeev off at the alley leading to his house. Still, Gaurau insisted that we stop by and see his house and garden. "It's too late for lunch with Mr. Srivastava," Gaurau reasoned. "Besides, his temple worships at six. He won't be home."

The lights were out all over the neighborhood, so we had to view Gaurau's bright tropical flowers by the beam of his flashlight. His largest and most impressive plant was a slender tree sapling, the name of which I have already forgotten, but I cannot forget that he said, "We worship this tree. It is god."

I could not resist the temptation to pose the question burning in my brain. "Hindus have many gods," I began.

"Yes, Hindus have many gods," agreed Gaurau with an air of pride and enthusiasm.

"So my question is, 'What is a god?'"

"What is a god?" he repeated in a tone of mild shock. This was probably a heretical question that devout middle class Hindus would not think of asking.

"Yes, what is a god?" I persisted ingenuously. After all, being a foreigner, I could hardly be expected to know any better.

After a pause, Gaurau said, "God is the spirit that lives in everything. God is the mystery that creates and sustains the universe."

"That is the same god I believe in," I said eagerly. I was trying to think of a polite way to ask how this very Unitarian concept of God could be understood in terms of the huge pantheon to which we had just been introduced. I was toying with the theory that each of the various gods might represent a different value within the society. However, at that moment our conversation was cut short by the deafening grumble of an engine, presumably an awakening generator, as a bright light suddenly illuminated the courtyard, and Gaurau's mother appeared inviting us for tea. I was swamped with another wave of guilt about standing up Sant Doss on his two-thirty invitation for a delicious lunch prepared by his mother.

* * * * *

Another wave of guilt swamps me now in deja vu as I sit in the tea stall our first day of cycling, and I remember that we are again late for lunch with Sant Doss. I try to think of a polite segue into leaving.

Suddenly the young man at the counter watching the bike scolds and waves his fists at a crowd of teenage boys swarming around it. One of the boys sounds our warning bell while others play with the brakes and gear shift levers. When another boy starts to climb up into the front seat, our host jumps up and joins in the scolding.

The boys back off a bit away from the bike. Our host shakes his head. "I'm sorry they are so wild. Most of them have never seen an Englishman." I am not sure who all is included in the label, Englishman, but I presume he means all persons of European descent.

Dick stands up and hands the young man his tea glass. "It's okay. They haven't hurt anything," he says. "But we really should go. Thanks for the tea. By the way, would you happen to know where the Sundaram Restaurant is?"

"Yes, Sir," he replies without hesitation. "But it is called Sundaram Hotel. It is half kilometer from here. I bring my motorcycle. Show you the way."

CHAPTER 5

The Saint of Agra

We catch up with Sant Doss leaning on his motorcycle in front of the Sundaram Hotel. A wide grin crosses out his expression of amused exasperation and tenderness for these two crazy old foreigners. I want to give him a hug. But yesterday when I asked whether hugging is customary in India, he said, "In India we don't hug!" Come to think of it, recalling family scenes I had viewed through the windows of the Punjab Mail train, I could not recall anyone hugging their departing loved ones. In any case, the message is clear, Sant Doss doesn't want to be hugged. He is with his friends, Laura and Paule, a young Croatian couple who admire Sant Doss with loving looks and praise, but there is no hugging.

"Where have you been?" chides Sant Doss. "Did your wheel come off the trailer again, or was it another flat tire?"

"We were lost," I say.

"How could you get lost? You just go straight, no turns," he laughs.

"We weren't lost. Someone invited us for chai," protests Dick.

"That's what you were doing the other day when Mrs. Srivastava was waiting several hours with your lunch ready," said Laura. "Do Americans customarily stop for tea on their way to lunch?"

"Come, we must eat. I am very hungry," says Sant Doss still grinning through his mild impatience. He wears the same dignified sport jacket and red tie he had been wearing in our hotel room the night we arrived in Agra. Although we had not expected anyone, there he was standing at our door a few minutes after our arrival.

* * * *

He had bounded into the room on a swell of enthusiasm. When he opened his mouth to say, "Welcome to Agra, my friends, I am Sant Doss Srivastava from Servas, most honored to meet you!" several teeth seemed to be missing. He squinted at us through half inch thick spectacles and through strands of slick black hair hanging straight from the bald spot at the top of his head. It was love at first sight for us. Maybe it was our relief to finally meet someone from Servas, a fellow peace activist with whom we would have something in common.

We were already occupying the only two chairs, so Sant Doss sat down on the edge of the bed directly in front of us.

"So you will bicycle for peace across India! India will love you!"

"We are also promoting world parliament," I said. "We believe that is the only way to create a peaceful world order."

"So true! How could anyone deny it?"

"It's a hard sell in some circles."

"Not in India! You will find many people open to this. Democracy has helped create peace in India."

"We believe democracy in the international arena would have a democratizing effect upon all levels of society," said Dick.

Sant Doss nodded eagerly. "For certain!," he said.

A porter brought in a tray with three cups of chai. Even though Sant Doss had come in after we ordered the tea, the proprietor must have assumed we would need a third cup for our visitor. "Tomorrow Mr. Singh will bring you by my house on the way to your tour of the temples and Taj Mahal," said Sant Doss. "You will leave your luggage at my house while you tour with Mr. Singh. My mother will have lunch ready when you return. Afterwards we go to the press and the television station."

"That's great!" said Dick. "We need press coverage."

"Of course! If you don't tell your story, you have come all this way for nothing."

"I reached in my pack and took out one of our brochures for Sant Doss. He paused to read it carefully while sipping his tea. Then he said, "May I keep this? We will show it to the press," and stuffed it into his lapel pocket.

The second time I had seen Sant Doss was when we arrived at his home after Gaurau and Senjeev's tour of Agra and the Taj Mahal. It was well after dark. We were unequivocally late for lunch. Grinning at us just as he is now through an expression of mild impatience, he had bowed with palms together and said, "Namaste."

We bowed and returned the traditional Indian salutation, "Namaste."

We're so sorry to be late," I said. "But we were not in charge of the tour schedule."

"Oh, it's all right. Come sit down. We'll have tea and cookies."

It crossed my mind that I had not eaten any real food yet that day, only sweet chai, cookies, and candy. As if reading my mind, Sant Doss looked at me and said, "My mother will prepare dinner later. She had lunch ready for you at two o'clock. She was very disappointed that you did not come."

"We're so sorry," I apologized again. It was Sant Doss' mother who had greeted us in the morning when we dropped off the luggage. Draped in brown sari and veils, she had used a walker to ambulate her short round figure out to the edge of the parapet above. She had smiled down on us lovingly and had spoken Hindi to Gaurau in good natured tones. He had translated that we were most welcome and should store the luggage in the entry way. This would be an ideal place for Dick to assemble the bike. Its stone tile flooring would be easy to clean.

The adjoining room where we gathered for tea, and later slept, was a long narrow space with a single bed adjacent to each of the two main walls. Between the beds was a small wicker coffee table that looked more like a stool and two matching chairs. At the far end of the room there was a big screen TV set. This room did have a big window in the outer wall, but that was thickly draped.

While we were having tea, several friends gathered to meet us. A large important looking man, whose name I have forgotten, was introduced to us as the director of a telecommunications company.

He was incredulous when we told him we planned to bicycle to Bombay. "No! It is impossible to ride a bicycle to Mumbai. The roads are very bad!"

Dick showed him the map. "We plan to take secondary roads," he said.

"The secondary roads are even worse!" The man kept shaking his head as though he thought we must be insane.

After the telecommunications director left, a sweet young Croatian couple named Laura and Paule arrived. Dressed in jeans and T-shirts, they seemed like typical well traveled European students. Laura had brought with her one of our *Bike for Global Democracy* brochures. She fingered it nervously with one hand while holding her tea cup with the other. "I have been reading this interesting brochure. I want to know why you think a world parliament would create peace."

"We are followers of Gandhi," I say. "He believed that the peoples of the world must be united as one family and working together for the common good. That is the only way to end war."

"That would be great if it would work." Laura's lips curled in an expression of skepticism.

"A good model to think of is the European Parliament," said Dick. "Europeans had been killing each other off in wars for hundreds of years, but now as more and more countries become embedded in this larger democratic structure, war between these countries becomes unlikely."

"It would be hard to imagine the State of Rajasthan going to war with Maharashtra. They are embedded in a larger democratic structure." put in Sant Doss.

I looked at Sant Doss with increasing admiration. He already knew my lines before I said them. "Right! Or California going to war with Oregon."

"Then you are for world government," concluded Paule.

"That's not the point," I said. "We already have world government. There are all these institutions running the world. There's the World Bank, the International Monetary Fund, the United Nations Security Council, and so forth. But none of them are elected by the people."

"This is rather idealistic," laughed Paule.

"Yes, democracy is idealistic," agreed Sant Doss. "Churchill said democracy is the worst form of government except for all the others."

Everyone laughed as if Sant Doss had the last word, but then Laura objected. "Democracies, like most other governments, are so corrupt. Whenever the government tries to do something good for people someone's greed messes things up."

"Like with your scholarship," said Paule.

"Yes, someone at the University is embezzling the scholarship money for foreign students. We are supposed to be paid a certain amount of money per month. Instead we get less than half of what we were promised. We cannot afford to live on that, so I may have to give up my school program."

"Did you go to the administration office and talk to them about it?" Sant Doss asked.

"Yes, I asked them to show me the contract papers like you said. I could even see where they had altered the figures, crossing zeros off the numbers. They are very crooked."

"Then you must go to the press. I will take you there. I know people in the press office," declared Sant Doss.

Laura's expression changed from disgust to fear, then to resignation. "All right, but we have to wait until after they post the examination results on Thursday. Otherwise they might retaliate by lowering my marks. After Friday, it doesn't matter. I will have to go back home if they don't give me more money anyway."

Sant Doss stood up and spelled out the program, "Tomorrow I will take Mona to the press office while Dick puts together their bicycle. Wednesday we will all ride with Dick and Mona on their first day of cycling toward Bombay. We will all stop together at Fetehpur Sikri and visit the ancient walled city and the Palace. Thursday when Dick and Mona are gone, I will take Laura to the press. But now I am hungry. I will go upstairs and see whether my mother has dinner ready. "

Everyone smiled at Sant Doss as he left the room.

"Sant Doss is an amazing guy," said Dick.

"Yes Sant Doss is a wonderful person," Laura agreed. "Even

though he has very little himself, he has given Paule and me all the furnishings and utensils for our apartment. He says he doesn't need a lot of things."

"With greed and corruption so widespread in the world," I said. "We are lucky to have found this patron Saint so aptly named, Sant Doss, to look out for us."

* * * *

Next morning after breakfast, I had some questions for Sant Doss. "Where's the waste basket?" I asked.

He wrinkled his nose and wobbled his head from side to side in confusion at the sight of the jumble I held in my hand. There were a couple of cough drop wrappers, a Kleenex, a length of dental floss, an envelope. He motioned to the side of the wall in the entry way. "Put it there," he said. "The maid will be here in a few minutes."

With some misgivings, I obeyed. At least he didn't insist, as had the woman on the train, that I throw things out the window.

"Sure," I said, "Thanks. Oh yes, another question. How to do laundry?" Our limited supply of clothing was filthy after a week of travel. I wanted to at least begin bicycling with clean clothes.

Sant Doss peered at me through squinted eyes as if questioning my intelligence. Was it possible that a woman my age didn't know how to do laundry? "There is a big bucket and a bar of soap in the bathroom. You can hang them to dry on the roof," he said.

That was how I learned the system for doing laundry in India. For some stupid reason, it had never occurred to me that there would be no Laundromats or washing machines. Of course, I knew about the bucket and soap. I had just used them to wash my bottom. It had never once occurred to me that they performed collateral duty as the family laundry.

The maid came in while I was gathering up our laundry. At least I assumed this was the maid although Sant Doss did not introduce her. She was an attractive young woman in a beautiful soft sari with transparent veil. From the start, it was plain to see that her job description was a little different from that of the Merry Maids who used to swirl through our house like tornadoes wielding their vacuum cleaners and feather dusters leaving it sterile within minutes. Instead, this maid stood in the entry way for quite awhile giggling and talking with Sant Doss. Then she grabbed the TV remote control from his hand and switched the channel from his news program to sexy popular music videos. As I climbed the white tile staircase with my pack of laundry, I could still hear Sant Doss and the maid giggling together in front of the television.

To get to the bathroom, I had to pass through Sant Doss' mother's room. By this time, I had figured out that the sitting room below was normally where Sant Doss slept but he had given it up for us. His mother's room was furnished similarly with two single beds and a small set of wicker table and chairs. Off that room were two dark closet sized rooms which served as kitchen and bathroom. As I passed through with my pack of laundry toward the bathroom, I saw Sant Doss' mother seated on the stone tile floor chopping vegetables for our lunch. There was no cutting board, just the floor.

Later while pinning laundry to a clothes line on the roof terrace, I noticed the maid squatting in the corner by a large metal bowl washing dishes. We smiled and greeted one another. I was wearing my long black skirt and colorful bicycle jersey because everything else was in the wash. It was pleasant to be open to the sky after spending so much time in the dark windowless bathroom doing the wash, rinsing everything twice and wringing out each item of clothing separately. I have always been more sensitive to cold than heat, so it felt good to be damp and sweaty in the morning sunshine.

From this vantage point, I could see most of the semi-walled compound where members of Sant Doss' temple community lived together. The houses were built adjacent to one another with no yards, but they all had roof terraces like this one. Some of the terraces contained potted plants or even vegetable gardens overlooked by windows. A few of the other roofs were also inhabited by women doing laundry, washing dishes, chopping vegetables. The clay streets below were pot holed and rutted, but there was not much litter. Before I was finished hanging the laundry, Sant Doss appeared. "We have to go," he said. "It's time for your interview at the press office."

As I followed Sant Doss out through the entry way, we said goodbye to Dick who was intently screwing bike parts together. His pile of metal tubes and wheels was beginning to take the shape of a bicycle.

When we got out into the street, Sant Doss put on his motor-cycle helmet. That was when it dawned on me by what method of transportation we were to arrive at the press office. It had been at least three or four decades since I had boarded a motorcycle, and at that time I had been wearing jeans. So here I was with a full length skirt dangling around my heels, and there was Sant Doss waiting expectantly on his motorcycle like it was the most ordinary every day occurrence for an old lady in a floor length dress to hop on behind.

So I did. I pulled the skirt up to about knee level and straddled the seat behind Sant Doss. Whereupon we darted off down the street. With white knuckles, I reached around Sant Doss' chest and grabbed his lapels. I presumed that was how I was supposed to keep myself on the thing. There were no other obvious handles.

I felt like a knight going into battle without his armor as Sant Doss charged through the streets, jousting with oncoming motor-cycles and taxis. I was wishing I had at least worn my bicycle helmet when Sant Doss darted between three bicycles and an oncoming camel cart. I let out a gasp of terror to which Sant Doss calmly responded, "Not to worry. I am twenty five years doing this." That was somewhat reassuring, but even so, a quarter of a century of amazing luck does not necessarily guarantee one more day.

When we got to the newspaper office, Sant Doss stalked up to the front desk and spoke to the sari clad receptionist in rapid Hindi. Then he marched me into the inner office as though he owned the place. Inside, there was a large conference table where several dark handsome men in impeccable suits sat around having their mid-morning chai. These were, by far, the best dressed Indians I had seen yet. They invited us to sit down and join them for tea. As we sat down, Sant Doss explained to me that this was not the interview. We would just visit with these gentlemen and have tea while we waited for the reporter. It was good that he clarified this. It seemed like an interview or at least a friendly interrogation.

"What is your opinion of your government's war policy?" demanded the handsomest, best dressed gentleman seated at the head of the table. I presumed this to be the editor.

"As Mr. Srivastava has told you, I am a follower of Gandhi. Gandhi has taught us that war is not the way. There is a better way."

They looked at me in wide eyed astonishment. "Do you not agree with your leaders then?"

"No," I said. "But I am not alone. Many Americans do not agree with them."

"Then what must be done about terrorism?"

"I don't know," I admitted. "But the war policy makes more enemies and therefore more terrorists. Gandhi would advise our leaders to look within themselves and remove the terrorism from their own hearts. After that, they will have open minds capable of hearing people describe the true causes of terrorism."

Clearly dissatisfied with my answer, the editor knitted his brow into a frown. Then he took a very deep breath and let it whistle back out through his teeth. Meanwhile, the other men all nodded and smiled.

When the reporter arrived, the gentlemen all left me and Sant Doss alone with her at the conference table.

I took an immediate liking to the reporter who introduced herself as Sara. She had a kind, attentive manner and seemed to return my admiration. This was my first conversation with an Indian woman who wore neither veil, nor dupatta, nor sari. In fact, she was dressed very much like I would on a normal day in tan slacks and a T-shirt, sensible attire suitable for a long day of fast paced hard work. "So why are you cycling to Mumbai?" she asked.

"Bicycling is a good way to see the country side and interact with real people," I said. "If you go someplace on a bicycle, it feels like you have really been there. We want to tell people about global democracy as the way to bring peace. My husband and I hope to do this all over the world."

"Why have you chosen India at this time?"

"India is the world's largest democracy," I said. "We will end up in Bombay at the World Social Forum where we will help organize a coalition to promote world parliament."

The interview lasted about one hour. Sara was a good listener who seemed to approve of my every word. At the end of the hour, she promised to come to Sant Doss' house that evening to take a picture of Dick and me on the bike.

After we left the newspaper office, Sant Doss took me to the television station. He led me to a chair upon which were trained a number of spot lights and cameras. That was when it dawned on me that I was about to be in a televised interview.

"Did you bring a comb?" Sant Doss reminded. I probably looked a bit wind blown after the motorcycle ride.

* * * *

We left Agra bleary eyed at five AM next morning, a good hour before sunrise. The plan was to get out of Agra before the traffic got too heavy with Sant Doss leading the way on his motorcycle, Laura and Paule both perched on the seat behind.

I had thought the plan timid enough. I guess I had imagined five o'clock in Seattle with its quiet deserted streets, but such was not true of Agra. There was traffic, not as much as at midday but every bit as heavy as rush hour on a minor cross town arterial in Seattle. Many of the oncoming vehicles were taxis with head lights so we were at all times at least partially visible to the many people who were everywhere, strolling along in the roadway, wrapped up in blankets, lying on the edge of streets or huddled over fires. People would blink at us in shock through their early morning stupors as if they thought they must be still asleep and dreaming. The air was thick with smells of auto exhaust, chemical smoke, and poverty.

Adding to the sense of chaos was the fact that we had not the slightest idea where we were going. We only knew that we were supposed to follow Sant Doss' motorcycle whereever it went. This might have been simple enough had there been a low speed or any functioning tail light on Sant Doss' vehicle. Given the circumstances, however, our target was pretty hard to hit. Paule had assured us that he would be always on the lookout for us and would not let us get lost. Whenever we had given up hope of ever seeing our friends again, Paule's white scarf and Laura's yellow windbreaker would materialize out of the void as they stood beside the road flagging us down.

Each time we stopped it was at a newsstand still closed up for the night. Sant Doss would run around calling out to people and banging on metal doors. It took me awhile to figure out that he was trying desperately to roust someone out to sell him a morning paper. It was already dawn when Sant Doss managed to obtain the object of his quest, a copy of the morning paper with a front page photo of me and Dick on our bike.

* * * *

We are sitting at the Sundaram Hotel having our last meal of vegetable biryani and dahl with Sant Doss, Laura and Paule. After visiting the Fatehpur Sirkri Palace a few miles down the road, we will take off to the south alone while they motorcycle back to Agra. We may never see them again. Yet they feel like family to me after knowing them for only a couple of days. I guess that goes with the *Bike for Global Democracy* territory. It was a feeling I experienced often on our last trip up the U.S. coastline from Miami to Maine.

While I entertain melancholy thoughts, Sant Doss is making other plans. "When we get to Fatehpur Sirkri, I will watch the bikes while the four of you tour the Palace," he says.

"No, you should go in with us," I object. "You will miss out on the fun." Actually, what I really mean is that I will miss the fun of having him along.

"I have seen Fatehpur many times. I will see it many times again. You may not come back again ever. It will be much safer to have someone with the bikes."

"It must be wonderful if you go there so often," I say.

Mona and Dick in the courtyard of Fatehpur.

"They say it is very beautiful and completely restored," says Laura who is a student of Sanskrit and Indian history. It was a fortified city built by Akbar, the great Mogul ruler in the 16th Century. Akbar was a very enlightened ruler. He wanted to promote religious tolerance, so his three principle wives were of different faiths—Christian, Muslim, and Hindu. He tried to create a new religion comprised of all three."

"Is that why you come so often?" I ask Sant Doss.

"All my Servas guests want to see it, so I come with them," he says.

As we approach Fatehpur, I snap a photo outside of Sant Doss, Laura, and Paule. Inside, Laura takes a picture of Dick and me with a huge expanse of red stone courtyard and palace in the background. I wish we could have all been in it together. In a few short minutes, our patron Sant Doss and this supportive little family will be gone. Dick and I will be on our own in rural India.

Laura, Paule, and Sant Doss outside Fatehpur Sirkri.

CHAPTER 6

Police Encounters

Bicycling in India is far better than we had expected. So far, we have encountered virtually no hills as we skim along the far left of the black top headed for the small town of Bayana in the state of Rajasthan. In mid afternoon on this December day, it is 80 degrees Fahrenheit, perfect temperature for a thermally impaired old lady. We are told not to expect a drop of rain at this time of year.

Women in saris bend low over wheat fields and rice paddies working with bare hands or short handled tools. Off in the distance, brown hills rise from irrigated farmland graced with charming huddles of haystacks and grass roofed huts. Herbal aromas mixed with dung tease the heavy air as we pass miles of sunny yellow mustard fields bordered with pink and purple wild flowers. Even though every pore of my skin is clogged with dirt, and it is difficult to see through the dust on my spectacles, it crosses my mind that I might actually like being a poor farmer. Imagine never being cold!

As we pass a row of scrubby misshapen trees, I notice a woman standing on one of their limbs, her sari blowing in the breeze. She steadies herself by holding onto the trunk with one arm while chopping off a higher branch. Several other women walk along the shoulder of the road balancing on their heads huge metal bowls crowned with stacks of firewood taller than themselves. The practice must be to cut off limbs for firewood, mercifully preserving the life of trees while leaving them looking deformed as thalidomide victims.

During a roadside break, I have a chance to examine the wild flowers as I huddle behind a bush to take a leak. One common variety has large pink trumpet flowers, much like morning glories with glossy heart shaped leaves hung from thick woody vines. Another has sprays of purple blooms the shape of onion domes on local temples. Because toilet paper is scarce in India and because there would be no place to dispose of it anyway, I use the leaves of these plants to wipe.

The best part of cycling in India is that we are by no means the slowest critter on this road. Motorized vehicles are accustomed to going around the likes of us. Cows wander across the pavement in

Dick pushes the bike past local women carrying bowls of sticks for firewood.

groups of three or four or more. People walk in the roadway pushing big carts of vegetables already spread out for sale at the nearest village market. Camel carts and teams of oxen are more common than private automobiles. Most people travel the roads by bus or jitney for which women in saris and men in dhotis wait with bundles at cross roads. Young men on motorcycles, some with veiled wives

Dick pushes the bike through an Indian village on our route.

on behind, pull up beside to ask where we're from. Most of the time, a few of the pedal powered variety draft in our wake.

One teenaged cyclist pulls up from behind and tries to converse. "You are from what country?"

"America."

"America? Where made your cycle?"

"Oregon. A company called Bike Friday," says Dick.

The boy taps my white plastic water bottle, an unknown phenomenon in rural India. "Petrol?" he asks.

"No, it's water," I assure him. One of the advantages of the stoker job is that my hands are always free. So I demonstrate by reaching down, pulling the bottle out of its cage and taking a drink.

The boy leers at the bike some more, then creases his brow and wobbles his head. "No engine?"

Dick looks back and grins, "Wife is engine," he says.

"Husband is big strong engine!" I boast.

The boy points to the bike, "What cost?" he demands.

"Expensive," I say.

The boy pedals quietly along beside me for awhile. Then he says, "Why no engine?"

Reading the silence between his remarks, I realize that it has never before occurred to this young man that someone who could afford a motorized vehicle would chose a bike instead.

The boy's head still wobbles in confusion as something big honks furiously from behind wanting to pass. The young man scurries off into the rocky dust of the shoulder as a colorfully painted truck roars around into the dirt on the opposite side. All the while, Dick doggedly stays his course at the left-hand edge of the pavement. I close my eyes as I often do when I don't like what's happening. I can still hear the truck's horn scolding like an insulted gander, as it roars off into the distance.

Although I am amazed at Dick's stubborn claim to the left-hand edge of the black top, I realize the importance of it. We can't afford many more flat tires. We should have invested in a mountain bike tandem with tires that would take the rocky shoulders. Our four inner tubes already look like patchwork quilts, and there are no tubes in India the correct size to replace them. Whenever we come into a village, we have to dismount and walk through it followed by mobs of people. For some reason there is no pavement inside villages. The entire roadway is bare with inches of dust and embedded rock. At first we had braved those conditions to evade pursuing crowds, but necessity has dictated that we choose mobs over flats.

The teenaged cyclist drops behind in our wake again while a large white SUV pulls up along side and slows down. Through its several open windows, middle aged male faces stare at us in consternation. They neither nod nor greet, just stare. I conjure up a faint smile and wave, but then I notice that they're all wearing olive green military style uniforms with army caps. As they pull ahead to go around us, I read the black logo on the side of their van. "It says Bayana Police Department." I call out to Dick as the van stops on the roadside up ahead. About half dozen police officers get out and walk into the roadway forming a blockade before us. The largest and most impressive officer waves a thick arm decorated with medals and gold braid.

What do they want with us? Had we unknowingly broken the law? One thing I have read about India is that you don't want to tangle with the police. They have been known to dole out swift and immediate justice. Maybe it's against the law for slow vehicles to hug the edge of the pavement and make everything else, no matter how big and fast, go around into the dust. In fact, someone had told us, facetiously we thought, that the biggest rig has the right of way.

The big one says, "I am Captain of the Regional Police Department traveling to Bayana. You are from what country?"

"America. U.S.A."

"Where are you going?"

"We're bicycling from Agra to Bombay," says Dick.

The vine covered bike walla stand where we repaired our flat tire.

I reach in the front pocket of my windbreaker and pull out our Agra newspaper clipping. I also hand him Sant Doss' letter asking for help to find lodging and food. "Today we're going to Bayana."

The police chief reads the article aloud to the others. They all nod and smile approvingly. The police chief hands me back the article and says, "Welcome to Rajasthan. When you reach Bayana, come to the police station. We will help you find a place to stay." The policemen all bow and say, "Namaste," then pile back into their SUV.

Dick and I stand in the road for awhile gazing at one another in shared relief as though a miracle had saved us from disaster. I offer a prayer of thanks to Ganesh and to the Universe as we remount. But Dick reminds me of our central concern. "If we have another flat tire today or take a wrong turn, we may not get to Bayana before dark," he says. When the temperature is 80 degrees, it's hard to remember that it is December and therefore gets dark at five-thirty. It is already four o'clock. The two flat tires in the morning had thrown us quite off schedule.

Fixing flats would not have taken so long had it not been for all the help. The first one popped by coincidence in front of a ramshackle bike wallah stand engulfed by a wide leafed vine with big red flowers. I took the bike wallah's picture in front of the stand, but Dick didn't solicit his services. Instead he turned the bike upside down and set it on a huge slab of stone nearby. While he worked, the inevitable crowd of teenage boys grew to almost unmanageable size, and Dick let them take turns pumping up tubes, putting them in pans of water to find leaks, scraping the leaks with sand paper. They had a great time. One of the boys tried on Dick's bicycle helmet over his red head-shawl. I took the boy's picture wearing a smug expression that said, "I'm so cool!"

The other flat occurred out in a farming community. A pipe gushed irrigation water out of a tank nearby a stone porch waiting

A young Indian poses in Dick's helmet over his red head-shawl.

in the shade to be used as a workshop. The crowd that gathered was the most respectful we have encountered so far. This was the first group yet to include girls. A pretty little girl of about twelve walked up to us carrying a big basket of straw on her head. She wore a dusty purple Punjabi dress with pajama like pants underneath. Without setting down her burden, she came up close and watched with intense curiosity. Another girl walked up balancing a big stainless steel water jug on her head. They looked so pretty in their dresses that I had to take their picture. When I showed them their images lit up on the digital camera screen, they got very excited and insisted upon showing everyone. After that, all the kids wanted their pictures taken. If flat tires force us to shorten our trip, they will have created a lot fun in the meantime.

Fortunately, the third and final flat tire of the day holds off until just after we reach the heart of Bayana. This town is relatively free of the usual blackened corrugated metal, broken cement, graffiti covered walls, and sundry ugliness of other small towns. There is an aura of tidiness about many of these red brick and concrete block houses lined up side by side along teeming streets. A woman leans

Young girls dressed in Punjabi dresses carrying loads on their heads.

out of her doorway sweeping litter away from the entrance. Even so, busy intersections are littered with trash. A layer of scum covers a mysterious gray-green puddle (the source of which is undetermined since it has not rained for months) reflecting the glow of fading sunlight. Crowds of people mill about oblivious of the dead dog lying in the roadway waiting to be finished off by pigs and other stray scavengers of its own species.

The instant we stop to change the tire, we are assaulted by a host of screaming little city urchins, dramatically different from the calm and pleasant country kids we had met earlier in the day. One of these has an especially irritating voice which seems to be firing up the rest who crowd in around Dick, clicking gear levers, turning pedal cranks, ringing bells, grabbing water bottles. They press in so close to us that we can't turn the bike over, let alone change the tire. I've noticed that every mob has its own distinct character which is determined by the personalities of at least one or two dominant leaders. A wealth of research data on mob psychology could be gleaned from a tandem bike trip across India.

Dick gives up on changing the tire. Instead he points around saying, "Police Thane?" asking directions to the station. Whereupon the mob leader lets out a piercing cry and runs up a shallow incline gesturing for us and the gang to follow. In a few minutes we are standing before a wrought iron fence surrounding a cobblestone courtyard. As we enter through a wide gateway, the children wait outside watching in silence. A policeman comes out through another gateway and says, "Welcome to Bayana. Please come in." As we follow the policeman into another courtyard, I glance back and see that the hundred or so children are joined by dozens more adults all gaping at us in wonder. It feels like a movie in which we aliens from another planet have said, "Take me to your leader."

As if this day had not yet produced enough stressors, a big one greets us inside the courtyard. The entire area is covered with rows of folding chairs facing a microphone and speakers platform. The policeman helps us park the bike, then leads us to the front of the platform and motions toward a row of chairs facing out toward the audience. People gather and rapidly fill all the chairs. We could not be more conspicuous, two strange looking white headed creatures in loud bicycle jerseys facing a room full of dark handsome males of all ages. Some of them wear traditional Indian clothing, dhotis, robes, or turbans. Others are dressed in slacks and cotton shirts, but there are also a few pairs of blue jeans. Everyone looks at us. What else can they do? Besides a litter of blonde shorthaired puppies curled up asleep on the platform, we are "It" at the moment. I have no idea why we're here. This looks like some sort of press conference. Are all these people going to interview us? The press and TV offices in Agra had been fairly innocuous compared with this.

Several young police officers in casual cotton uniforms come in with trays of chai glasses. First they serve Dick and me and then start moving about the room offering tea to everyone. People chat with one another while drinking their tea. No one says anything to us, but some have not taken their eyes off us yet. They are waiting for something. I have no idea what. After an eternity or so, in comes the regional police chief we had met on the road. He takes center stage and begins to speak Hindi into the microphone. After awhile he concludes his speech and people start asking him questions. By this time, I have figured out that the police chief is the one on the hot seat, not us. I cannot, of course, understand a single word, but the situation finally makes sense. The citizenry is confronting the visiting regional police chief with complaints and concerns about police services. Dick and I have been given front row seats to observe Indian democracy in action. Although some of the questioners use angry tones, and people seem generally dissatisfied, everyone is basically civil. They are working things out. This much I can tell without understanding one syllable.

As the meeting drones on into dusk, the puppies awaken and begin tumbling over one another in play. A healthier than usual, but otherwise nondescript blonde specimen of Indian canine essence meanders in and flops down to feed her litter. I still don't know where we will eat or sleep tonight, but I sense that we are in adequate hands.

CHAPTER 7

Humble Accommodations

Two days out of Bayana, I sit on the edge of our bed in the Basant Hotel at Gangapur trying to catch up on my diary while Dick is out searching for an Internet cafe. He hopes to email Bike Friday and ask them to send some inner tubes to the Palm Grove Hotel in Chennai. Otherwise we may have to give up on this adventure. Besides a planned side trip by train to Chennai for the Seventh Provisional World Parliament in late December, we have no idea where we will stay on any given night.

Worse yet, I seem to be coming down with something. I have two mysterious symptoms. One is a nagging cough, and the other is total absence of appetite which for a lunch mouth like me is worrisome. I ate very little of our rice and lentils for dinner last night, and this morning I cannot convince my stomach to accept anything, not even a banana or a cup of tea. I don't know what I have, but for lack of a more definitive diagnosis, I will call it Basant Hotel Fever.

This room itself is enough to turn one's stomach. The air smells like a mixture of mold, cement dust, and urine. The decor is even worse. Long ago, someone must have sloshed paint over the upper half of the walls and let it dribble down onto the lower half. The paint is flaking off now and many layers of yellow dust have obscured its dubious green color. On top of that, someone has more recently smeared something brown and gooey like feces over everything including the toilet. The washing bucket and pitcher are likewise smeared with brown goo, and when you touch them, little pieces of plastic disintegrate into your hand. There is one window opening out onto the hallway, but the glass is so thickly coated with gray film that no curtain is needed. On the wall opposite the window a crumbling travel poster is barely discernible through the screen of dust. There is an English inscription but the words are so obscured by dust that only one of them is legible. Ironically, that *only* decipherable word happens to be *only*.

While I try to write, the one light bulb goes out and the ceiling fan stops. It is mid morning now, high time for the electricity to go off all over town.

I feel my way along the dark hallway out onto the balcony, which commands a view of the rutted unpaved street below. Hundreds of people scurry about, walking or using a variety of transportation — bicycles, camel carts, and motorized and human-powered rickshaws. I wave joyfully when two women wearing saris ride by on bicycles.

I missed the women cyclists but snapped this camel instead from my hotel room.

These are the first women cyclists I have seen, so I rush back in for the camera, but they are gone by the time I get back. Instead I snap a photo of a passing camel cart.

Out in the haze, I cough even more but begin to relax as persistent rays of sun penetrate the heavy layer of air pollution and finally reach my brain. The hotel manager, a handsome gentleman, tall by Indian standards, comes out onto the balcony bringing two plastic chairs. "Madame would like breakfast?" he asks.

I pat my stomach. "No, thank you. I am sick."

"Water, Madame?"

I thoughtfully consider this offer. I am indeed thirsty. My stomach would accept water, but I wonder whether that may be the cause of at least one of my symptoms. I had seen the water's dubious source in the dark entryway below, where the manager and several other young men sit throughout the day watching television. Beside the TV set is a big jug from which they had dipped water into our glasses. Peering into the jug, I had spotted a layer of scum and dust floating on the surface.

"Do you have bottled water?" I ask.

The manager's head wobbles in confusion.

"Bottled water. Aquafina!" I take a page from my diary and draw a picture of a tall bottle labeled *Aquafina*.

The man peers at my illustration, shakes his head, and points down into the street. "Market," he says.

Dick comes out onto the balcony. "Let's have tea now," he says. "Then we can go through the market on our way out of town and buy some bottled water."

I let Dick drink both our glasses of chai while he studies the map. "Since our tires won't hold up, maybe we should ship the tandem home and just use single local bikes for the remainder of the trip," I suggest.

Dick shakes his head. "We wouldn't make it to Bombay in time for the World Social Forum. But I think we may be okay anyway. These are pinch flats we've been getting from the wheels pressing against the tubes. I've padded the metal edges with tape and lowered the pressure a little. We just have to get off and walk when there's no pavement and avoid the worst bumps."

"How far will we try to go today?"

He shows me the map. "The next town of any size is Sawai Modophur, but that's over a hundred kilometers. So we'll be staying tonight at a village with no hotel. We'll have to show people our newspaper articles and get somebody to put us up."

My anxiety level begins to rise again. Here I am feeling sick and I don't know where we will spend the night. Actually I would prefer sleeping in a mustard field under our mosquito netting to this dingy hotel, but the thought of trying to sleep surrounded by an inevitable crowd of who knows how many on-lookers is unthinkable. Even when we break for a picnic lunch on the roadside way out in the country, dozens of people stop to watch us eat. In planning for the trip, we had tried to envision all eventualities, but the experience of being constantly pursued by crowds is something we could not have imagined.

The "Vishnu General Store" in Gangaphur.

In the market on our way out of Gangapur, we stop by a stall with a sign saying, "Vishnu General Store." Below the sign is a rusty corrugated metal awning heavily littered with scraps of paper, rope, bricks, and what looks like an old bicycle tire. From the awning an assortment of belts, handkerchiefs, and children's clothing hangs over stacks of boxes and shelves of shoes. Next to that is a mountain of bricks and a colorful three-tiered cart of fruit.

Dick waits with the bike surrounded by a human bulwark of more than a hundred young men while another dozen or so follow me around from stall to stall. Besides locating our usual samosas and bananas, I am delighted to discover a man standing over a huge kettle of boiling eggs. I hold up six fingers and point to the eggs. "What cost for six?" I ask.

"Ten rupees!"

I nod. "Six eggs, please."

The egg wallah takes a big stainless steel spoon, fishes one egg out of the pot, peels it and starts to roll it about in some goopy sauce. I shake my head vehemently. "No! In the shell." I gesture with cupped palms enclosing a circle. "In the shell!" I repeat.

The egg wallah looks at me quizzically, shrugs and wobbles his head, but nevertheless wraps the half dozen unpeeled eggs in old newspaper and secures the package with a length of black thread.

I am batting a thousand! But now for the hard stuff. I have run out of several essential items so, for the first time, I must approach an Indian small town market with a shopping list more suitable for Walgreen's. Jotted on a page torn out of my diary are a few of what I consider to be fairly humble necessities:

shampoo . . . cough drops . . . dental floss . . . kleenex . . . bottled water

I find a stall that seems, by its shelves of bottles and jars, to be a pharmacy. "Shampoo," I say acting out the scrubbing of my scalp. The vendor hands me a small shiny black plastic bottle sporting a picture of a woman with a generous head of radiant black hair. The brand name of this shampoo is, in fact, "Shiny Black." Hoping that it is only shampoo and does not contain any black pigments, I agree to pay three rupees for it. Then I cover my mouth, cough, and say, "cough drops."

The man nods and smiles total comprehension. "Cough drops!" he exclaims and hands me a long strip of separately wrapped small green candies, each labeled, "Vikas."

"Ah, yes! Vicks cough drops!" I'm batting a million! Now for something more challenging. I pantomime flossing my teeth and say, "Dental floss, thread to clean teeth."

The man looks at me as though I must be daft.

"Long thread to clean teeth," I persist. Maybe it's called something else in India.

Suddenly, the man's eyes light up in recognition. "Tongue cleaner!" he exclaims. I wait in suspense while the man searches his shelves. Soon he hands me something wrapped in clear plastic. Peering through the packaging, I see a stainless steel object vaguely resembling a shoehorn. But hanging from the shoehorn shape is a spray of sharp pointed pegs that might be used for gouging out the eyes of small animals being butchered. Surely no one puts this in their mouth!

Shaking my head emphatically, I have another idea of how I might yet win this game of charades. I set my package of boiled eggs on the counter top and remove the thread with which I proceed to demonstrate the art of flossing.

This gets a huge laugh from the crowd. Someone yells something in Hindi. Everyone laughs again. With an astonished look in his eye, the drug store wallah's head rocks back and forth like a dingy cut loose in a storm. He shoves the little butchering gadget in my face again. "Need tongue cleaner. No string to clean teeth!" he chides.

Various members of our audience look at one another, nod, and smile. "Good! Clean teeth!" They all agree.

I glance around at the circle of gap-toothed jack-o-lantern grins. They are dubiously qualified to make dental recommendations. There is scarcely a complete set of teeth in the crowd.

Next on my list is Kleenex. With some misgivings, I say, "Tissues," and pretend to blow my nose into my hand. The drug store wallah shakes his head. "No tissues."

Finally I say, "Bottled water," and pantomime drinking. He shakes his head again and points down the street.

Dogged by my mobile audience, I try a couple of other stalls that have cases of coke and soft drinks stacked in front. But no one has bottled water. Instead they offer me a free drink from a pitcher.

"Drinking water," everyone assures me.

I thank them and fill our water bottles but add some iodine pills from our first aid kit just in case.

We parade the bike out of town behind our self-appointed bugler, a gaily-painted truck sounding its multi-tonal horn. About a hundred children march behind, laughing and screaming all the way. I feel like the Pied Piper of Hamlin and imagine myself crying out to their parents, "Better call off your little darlings if you ever want to see them again!"

It is nearly noon by the time we are out of Gangapur and making time on the road. I have not eaten anything yet today except for a couple of disgusting lime-flavored Vikas cough drops. Never the less, I still feel no hunger. I must be pretty sick. Yet I pedal along easily in a sort of fever-induced hypnosis.

Dotting the brown and thirsty landscape are brittle gray bushes and deep dry gullies. As the day wears on, parched hills emerge bare and lonely in the distance. Bent over the handle bars and peering out sideways at this desolation, there suddenly appears before me a scene that might have been staged by a Hollywood director trying to portray the Sahara Dessert. Four or five emaciated camels stand or lounge around the centerpiece,

Camp of nomads with camels.

which is an Arabian style tent. In the foreground, several women in colorful saris and men in shaggy robes mill about a big camp-fire.

Stunned out of my stupor, I yell, "Dick! Photo op!" We stop and I jump off the bike. Proffering the camera, I bow toward the tent and say, "Namaste," thus requesting, to the best of my ability, the peoples' permission to take their picture. A woman nods and waves. People in India love to have their pictures taken. So I aim the camera and click. But when I turn around to get back on the bike, I am overwhelmed by a frantic mob of dirty, ragged children, palms up, wiggling their fingers open and shut like a hundred baby alligators jawing for food. "Baksheesh! Baksheesh!" they scream.

As we try to mount up, they close in around us, grabbing and pulling at our clothing. Two grown women join in the fray, also screaming for pay. Most of my money is kept in a pouch hanging from my bra and not easily accessible, so I plead with Dick, "They want to be paid for the photograph!"

Dick hands one of the women ten rupees, but the mob continues to scream and grab at us as we try to pedal away. Then I look down and notice our water bottle cages are empty. The bottles are gone. "They've taken our water bottles!" I shriek.

With an expression of shock and horror, Dick waves his fist in the air. "Give us back our water bottles!" he demands. But people just keep clawing at our clothing and screaming for more baksheesh.

"Please go," I beg him. The prospect of cycling with no water on this hot afternoon is pretty scary. But I am even more afraid of what else might happen if we hang around here much longer.

After we have gone about a quarter of a mile farther, a young man pulls up beside us on a motorcycle. He is strikingly handsome and dressed in slacks and a clean tan windbreaker. This is a welcome sight because we have figured out that traveling by motorcycle in clean western style clothing is proof of middle class respectability on Indian roads. "You have a problem?" says the young man.

We stop and I point at our empty water bottle cages and then at the encampment back down the road. "Those kids stole our water," I moan.

The young man looks at us with kind, soulful eyes. "Wait just a moment. Someone will bring them." There is a soothing spiritual presence about him, like Jesus preparing to touch a leper and heal his wounds.

We look back down the road and, sure enough, someone is walking toward us with white cylinders dangling from the ends of his or her arms. Dick holds up the bike and converses with the beautiful young man while I walk back to meet the person bringing our bottles. I recall that the other day a teenaged cyclist had mistaken our water bottles for containers of petrol. The kids probably grabbed them more out of curiosity than meanness.

This time to be ready with a reward for the person returning our water, I reach in the little pouch under my shirt and pull out another ten rupee note. By now the person is close enough to discern his sex. It is a toothless elderly man wearing a frayed and dusty white robe. He is barefoot. At the sight of him, I wish that I had come up with a larger amount than ten rupees. In fact, after I hand him the money, the man starts to make grabbing motions with his hands as if he wants more, so I feel around in my pants pocket and luckily find a few more coins.

When I get back to the bike, Dick is still conversing with the young man. They are looking at our growing collection of Hindi newspaper articles with photos of us passing through different towns. They shake hands and smile at one another in a way that says they are fast friends.

After we are underway again, Dick says, "That was a great guy. His name is Kamlesh Tiwari. He really admires our mission. He says those people in the camp were a group of nomads. There are some in Rajasthan that wander about and survive mostly by thieving and begging."

"I hope there aren't any more of them up ahead." I wonder where we will stay tonight, imagining the unpleasant prospect of sharing an encampment with a bunch of unsavory nomads.

"Oh, by the way, not to worry about lodging tonight. Kamlesh said his uncle's family lives in the village of Malarna Dungar. We can stay with his cousin tonight, then tomorrow we'll visit his parents in Sawai Modophur."

"Wow!" Things are looking up. The prospect of two nights in a row with no concern about where to seek shelter is immensely relieving. Besides, Dick's new tire method seems to be working. We haven't had a flat all day.

But even so, I worry. "How will we find the cousin? Did Mr. Tiwari give you an address?"

"No. Kamlesh will phone ahead and say we're coming. He wrote down the name and said just to show it to someone as we enter the village. Everyone knows his relatives and will take us right to them.

"That's terrific!" I say. So why won't I stop worrying as I cough into my last Kleenex brought from home? It is late afternoon, and I still have not been able to eat anything all day.

CHAPTER 8

Interesting Conversations, Few Words

It is after sunset and well into dusk when, trail-worn and weary, we spot the small white village of Malarna Dungar nestled at the base of a mountain. As we pedal closer, we can see a staircase leading all the way up to a temple on the mountaintop. This is the most charming and picturesque part of India we have yet seen. By the time we dismount at the edge of town, it is almost dark. Perhaps that is why we are not greeted by dozens of screaming street urchins. It must be past their bedtime. In fact, the streets are amazingly deserted for an Indian village.

As we look about for someone to ask the whereabouts of Mr. Tiwari, a young man approaches on a motorcycle and motions for us to follow him. It's as if he has been watching and waiting for us. After all, there would be little chance of failure to recognize us. It's likely that we are the only elderly white couple to have entered this village by "doublecycle," as they call it, in the thousand or so years of its history.

We follow the motorcycle off the main road onto a dirt and stone pathway. We cross a ditch or slough of murky gray water, its greasy film reflecting the fading light. Two razor backed pigs cross our path, then turn and saunter up the hill in the same direction we are headed. We go up over a gentle rise and are amazed by the sight of a quaint little neighborhood reminiscent of a village in Greece or a scene from a textbook on the New Urbanism. There is a cluster of modest one and two story white stucco houses. Some are surrounded by gardens and low walls trimmed with decorative ironwork.

A man comes out of one house and introduces himself as Rakesh Tiwari, cousin of Kamlesh. He says he would be honored to have us spend the night in his home.

Rakesh's house has no wall around its garden. Instead there is a wide porch with exquisite stone-tile steps leading down onto the street. A young woman in long black braids and a royal blue Punjabi dress and smart black sweater is bent over the steps. Using a short handleless broom, she sweeps away at the thick layer of yellow dust that has spilled over from the road. Glancing about I notice that the walls surrounding the neighboring gardens are too low and unimposing to keep out humans or even animals. Rather these outer walls are meant as barriers to the relentless onslaught of dust. India is a paragon of freedom compared with South Africa and other parts of the world where homes and gardens are fortressed off by twelve-foot walls topped with razor wire.

Rakesh introduces the young woman as his wife while several neighbors come out of nearby houses also eager to be introduced. They are gorgeous Indian people of all ages, sizes, and shapes, but most of their exotic names flit in and out of my brain like little hummingbirds and disappear.

After the introduction ceremony, Rakesh ushers us, bike, trailer, and all through one of his two front doors into a small room containing an adequate sleeping cot made of woven plastic strips. The room is spotlessly clean. The cot looks comfortable enough to crash on this very minute and immediately lose consciousness, but that is not to be. Instead Rakesh tells us to freshen up and come into the adjoining room to meet the rest of his family and friends. I am not sure how we are meant to "freshen up," as there is no water in sight, and we have thick layers of dust glued with sweat to every inch of exposed skin. So I take off my sweaty bicycle jersey and tap into my dwindling supply of wet wipes to at least smear the dirt around a little. After that I go out into the adjoining room, which is simply

furnished and wonderfully clean with comfortable couches along
the walls. Dick is already seated there with Rakesh and two of his
friends engaging in the fine art of conversing when you don't have
more than a ten or fifteen word vocabulary in common.

What is your age?

How many children do you have?

What are the ages of your children?

What is your profession?

I have a more urgent question to ask Mrs. Tiwari on the side.
"Where is the toilet?"

She takes me out through a side door where there is a tiny toilet
stall at the end of a long veranda. Inside is the usual bucket of water,
pitcher, and hole. When I crouch over the hole, I notice bare ground
visible a few feet below. Also visible are the faces of two pigs waiting
to receive my offering. I am startled at this sight juxtaposed with a
tidy middle class life style. But I recall reading that the vast majority
of homes in India don't have plumbed-in toilets.

When I get back into the sitting room, Rakesh's son and several more neighbors have gathered. "Please sit, Madame," says
Rakesh, motioning for me to take the space on the couch between him and Dick. Rakesh holds his hand up, proudly displaying a gold leafed document certifying his business, The Tiwari
Trading Company, as an official distributor of fertilizers. He must
have brought this out with respect to the, "What is your profession?" topic. It is an interesting choice of conversation since the
question that constantly hangs in my brain when we travel along
roads anywhere in the world is, "What do all these people do for
a living?" We have noticed that a major difference between India
and America is that most Indians are self-employed, more or
less, but often less than more. I think about the many miles of
farmland we have passed. Rakesh has found a good niche.

"Is business good?" Dick asks.

Rakesh shrugs. "Not bad when the monsoons hold."

I recall speeches by the fiery Vandana Shiva at the World Summit
in Johannesburg espousing the benefits of natural sustainable farming
and cautioning against dependence upon oil-based chemicals. "What
kind of fertilizers do the farmers use?" I ask.

"Farmers use many kinds of homemade fertilizers. Our firm distributes chemical fertilizers." He flinches and glances away as though sensing my unspoken concern.

While we converse, Rakesh's son, a handsome, curly headed preschooler, climbs up on a cupboard beside the TV and plugs in some mysterious electrical box. Then he clambers down, snatches a remote control from the floor under the coffee table, and clicks on the set. "Saddam Hussein captured. Jubilant celebrations in Iraq," reads an English news release at the bottom of the screen.

All conversation stops. Everyone gasps. All eyes are now riveted on Dick and me as if to take advantage of this historic opportunity to experience firsthand how real live Americans would react to such news. "Jubilant celebrations, I'm sure," I murmur in a sarcastic tone. I glance sideways at Dick who also looks ill at ease.

"Are you not happy about this news?" asks Rakesh. "Will it not make your country victorious in the war?"

"We don't support the war," says Dick. "Besides, the capture of Saddam Hussein will make little difference. It won't stop the resistance."

Rakesh looks at Dick in shock.

"What your leaders should do to stop terrorists?"

Dick says, "Bombing people will not solve anything."

"What your leaders must do?"

Dick says, "We are followers of Gandhi. I believe Gandhi would say to focus on the welfare of the entire human family."

The corner of Rakesh's mouth curves upward in an expression of doubt. "Gandhi said to love your enemies. Can you do this? Is it possible to love enemies?"

Dick says, "I think so. At least it is possible to listen to their concerns. I think that is what Gandhi would advise."

Everyone nods and smiles as several neighbors leave and a third shift arrives to meet us. The newcomers have also heard the latest news, and Rakesh insists that Dick repeat for them what Gandhi would say about terrorism.

Among the new arrivals is a spunky, assertive teenage girl called

Laschmi who sits down beside me, dubs me "Auntie." and immediately lays claim to my undivided attention. This surprises me because back home old ladies like me are totally ignored by teenagers. "You are very strong, Auntie. You ride bicycle a long way across India." Lacshmi's English pronunciation is the most perfect I have yet heard in India. She must have rehearsed with a tape recording.

We start with the usual identification data, age, profession, number of children, but then Laschmi says something to Mrs. Tiwari in Hindi. Mrs. Tiwari makes agreeing noises, and Lacshmi stands, takes hold of my hand, and proclaims, "Tour, Auntie!" I have little choice but to arise and follow even though I am not sure what we are touring.

Our first stop is the Tiwari kitchen where I am invited to sit on the floor beside a slightly glorified version of a Coleman camp stove. Mrs. Tiwari comes in, sits down yoga style on the floor beside us and lights the stove. It puts out a cozy flame as I gaze about at white stucco walls that reflect a quaint, tasteful simplicity. An attractive display of useful utensils, pots, and pans of copper, wood, and pewter hang about from pegs of natural wood. Mrs. Tiwari takes a piece of dough from a bowl nearby and begins to flatten it out on what looks like a big cutting board. "Making chapatis," explains Lacshmi. I am fascinated with the process and hope to learn the rest, but Lacshmi gets up and takes my hand again, "More tour, Auntie," she says.

Lacshmi leads me out of the Tiwari home into her own house next door. This house is at least twice as large as the Tiwari's, and Lachsmi shows me every room, each as tidy as the one before. As with the Tiwari house, the floors are covered with artful stone tiles that seem to glow with pride at their achievement of staying so clean in a dust-filled world. Now I know the meaning of a tile company advertisement I had seen as we passed through one of the desolate streets of Gangapur. It was a small sign tied to a barbed wire fence that was stretched over a pile of rubbish. The sign read, *Create a world of your own—Gangapur Flooring*. It would be impossible to pick up all the trash in India. But nowhere in America have I seen tile flooring as magnificent as in modest Indian buildings. Maintaining one's sanity and happiness in a chaotic overpopulated society is simply a matter of not looking at anything until you get home. There, instead of ugliness and trash, you will find cleanliness and the exquisite beauty of *Gangapur Tiles*.

Lachsmi announces each room we enter as if rehearsing words for English class. "Bathroom! Toilet! Sleeping room! Basement! Kitchen!" In the kitchen, Lachsmi introduces me to her mother who stands at a western style gas range deep-frying puff bread. In contrast with the Tiwari's kitchen, everything here is designed for standing. There is even an upright refrigerator. But the next room takes us back into Indian style living, "Sitting room!" declares Lachsmi. She introduces me to her father who sits on the edge of a double bed watching a television set across the room. Lachsmi spreads an orange mandarin cloth the size of a double-bed sheet on the floor and invites me to sit. As soon as we are seated, several more teenage girls enter as if on cue. Beautifully attired in a tasteful mixture of Indian and western styles, they gather around cross-legged in a circle and look at me expectantly. It seems as though I am the evening's entertainment, and they are waiting for me to begin the program.

I start with the obvious.

What is your name?

How old are you?

They are too young to have a profession, so I have to think of something new. "What do you like to do?"

They stare at me blankly for a moment and then it is head wobbles all around. I'm not sure whether they didn't understand the question or don't know what they like to do or what. Could it be that they don't like to do anything? No, surely they must like something.

"Do you like reading?"

The heads all stop tilting and begin shaking from side to side. They don't like to read.

"Do you like sewing?" They look at me as if I am daft. It has never occurred to them that anyone might actually enjoy sewing.

I try running. They shake their heads.

Swimming? They wrinkle their noses and shudder in disgust.

Cooking? Definitely not!

Watching television? Everyone brightens, nods and smiles happy agreement.

I try several other activities hoping to come up with something worth doing besides watching the tube, but it's no use.

My next topic elicits even greater disdain. "When you grow up, what will you do for a career?"

A career? All heads wobble. Again it's hard to tell whether they understood my question. "What will you do for a job? For work?"

A job? Work? Now I must be really daft. Finally Lachsmi looks at me and, in clear precise English, replies, "No work. No job." The others agree by shaking their heads and repeating "No work. No job."

I am not certain whether "No work. No job," implies their total disdain for the idea of working for a living, or that their world offers no job opportunities, or both. However it seems clear that their most optimistic visions of the future are constricted to television soaps for housewives, provided there is a maid who does everything else.

Fortunately I don't have to try and come up with any more conversation topics for teenagers. Rakesh is at the door inviting me to come back to his house for dinner.

When I return to the Tiwari sitting room, all of the neighbors are gone. Rakesh is still there holding his son on his knee and listening to Dick explain why we need a world parliament. "Big corporations are global. So government by and for the people must be global," he explains. Each time he says the word, "global," Dick shapes a big sphere with his hands. Rakesh squints his eyes and wrinkles his brow thoughtfully.

Dick continues. "The parliament could start small, with a few countries." He moves his palms together, making the sphere smaller. India could be one of these few countries." Rakesh's eyes light up. He nods approvingly. Dick is doing a lot better than me at the making interesting conversation with a limited vocabulary. The lesser age difference clearly helps.

Mrs. Tiwari comes in with a tray of chapatis and lentils. When she sets the tray on the table in front of us, I note that there are only two plates. "Please have something to eat," she says and hands Dick and me each a plate. My stomach must have managed to solve whatever problem it was dealing with this morning because the food looks pretty appetizing. I am hungry enough to eat a fairly sizeable helping.

"Thank you so much. It looks delicious!" I exclaim. Still I cannot help but notice that this leaves no plates for anyone else. Oh well, we got here pretty late. Maybe the family had dinner before we came.

As Mrs. Tiwari leaves the room, I notice there are no knives or forks. There is a serving spoon in the lentil dish, so I spoon some lentils on a chapati and make a tidy little burrito to eat with my hand. It is spicy and delicious.

Meanwhile Dick has not stopped talking, but he is paying enough attention to follow my lead and make a generous lentil burrito for himself. All the while he expounds upon the World Social Forum we will attend in Bombay. "There will be thousands of people from all over the world," he says, gesturing with one hand while spooning lentils with the other. "We will have discussions about world parliament."

As we chew away on our burritos, I notice that Rakesh and his son are giving us strange looks while conversing together in Hindi. Out of their jumble of meaningless syllables, two distinct English words emerge. The two words are "Americans" and "sandwiches."

I blush crimson as my mind fills in the blanks between the two words and makes a sentence. *Americans like to eat sandwiches.* My imagination fills in more sentences, the lesson of a father trying to explain to his son why these two strange looking people have such weird eating habits. *Americans are foreigners and do not know the proper way to eat Indian food.* I feel anger emerging from my embarrassment. It was the guidebook's fault! It should have told us how to eat chapatis and lentils. Or was there something in there that I missed?

I vaguely remember something I had seen on the Punjab Mail train. It was Sharma's mother eating rice. She would tear off a bite-sized piece of chapati, wrap it like a delicate bird beak around a bit of rice, and put it in her mouth. I had thought it a peculiar habit of this one person, but that was before I had ever been served anything without a fork. Restaurants in Bombay had supplied forks, so had Sant Doss in Agra.

Mrs. Tiwari comes in and puts another chapati on my plate. Then she sits down on the couch across from us as if to watch us enjoying the results of her culinary skill. "*Kana bota acha hai!*" I recite a phrase carefully rehearsed to compliment the food. Everyone smiles appreciatively. Then I tear off a piece of chapati and use it to gather up a bite-sized clump of rice as Sharma's mother had done on the train. I glance around with my antenna up to discern any signs of embarrassment or disapproval. But everyone seems more relaxed now that at least one of their two visitors has figured out what to do with the food. Meanwhile Dick is still chatting away happily while making himself another burrito. I will translate for him later this wordless side conversation about table manners.

CHAPTER 9

The Tiwaris of Sawai Modhopur

The Tiwiari family in their rooftop garden.

This is the best laundry facility I have found, so far, in India. The Tiwari's home is located in a development known as the Housing

Board Colony, a government subsidized community on the out-skirts of Sawai Modhopur. Their simple home has an airy wash-room with a big skylight through which sunlight floods its white stucco walls. With my long black skirt hiked up at the waist, I stand barefoot on smooth stone tiles and let water spill over on them from the big earthenware bucket. Even after the second rinse, the water is still warm, its steam soothing my throat and nostrils far better than "Vikas" cough drops.

Over the past couple of weeks, I have worked out, by trial and error, a good wringing system. The first time at Sant Doss's house in Agra, I had struggled in vain to squeeze out enough water with my small bony hands. The result was that we had to start our first day of cycling in damp clothes. My new system is a cinch. The first step is to attach the article of clothing to a door or faucet handle and twist the two ends of cloth together over and over, braiding them into a sort of rope from which large quantities of water pour out. Next I fluff the garment out and roll it into a loose ball. Then I wrap a towel around the ball, set it on the floor and step on it several times, squeezing out most of the excess moisture. Because our bicy-cling jerseys and tan sports pants are made of nylon, they will then dry overnight.

As I twist one pant leg around the other creating a thick nylon rope attached to the door handle, the door suddenly opens, slack-ening the rope into a big letter U. Pryana, the youngest of Kamlesh's three sisters, a slender, graceful woman in her early twenties, stands in the doorway holding a small neighbor boy. The child clings to Pryana like a baby kangaroo in its pouch peering anxiously out at this weird stranger. They both look scrubbed and wholesome, the boy in western style trousers and T-shirt, Pryana in a blue Punjabi dress and gray wool sweater. As with so many Indian people, her beauty defies description. Pryana's long black hair cascades softly over her shoulders and her smooth olive skin and eyes reflect a quiet inner light.

"May we help, Auntie?" Pryana asks, looking sideways at my absurd U of braided trousers.

"Thanks. This is my last piece, but can you show me where to hang them?"

"Yes come. We go to the roof. We will help. Mother will have your tea ready soon."

After hanging the laundry, we come down the staircase leading from the roof to a tiny walled garden in front of the Tiwari home. A few tomato plants and two carefully tended rose bushes border a strip of grass smaller than the average American living room. The brick outer wall is no more than chest high, clearly meant more to deter dust and litter than any human or animal invader. In fact, Kamlesh's sister Rekhe stands at the open gate chatting with an older woman in Hindi. Dick and Mr. Tiwari are seated in a circle of molded plastic chairs on the grass. Mr. Tiwari holds one of our "Bike for Global Democracy" brochures. They are engrossed in a lively discussion about free trade.

"What would Gandhi say about the free trade system?" asks Mr. Tiwari.

Dick laughs. "I guess he would say, 'What free trade?' There is no such thing. How is it free when it has so many rules, all made by the rich countries who are the only ones that get to break the rules?"

At first Mr. Tiwari looks shocked, but then he grins knowingly. "The rich countries are allowed to protect their industries with tariffs and subsidies, but no one else can do this," he observes.

"Yes," says Dick, "And trade is in U.S. dollars, so poor countries have to borrow to engage in the system. Soon they end up in debt slavery."

I sit down in one of the empty chairs, but Pryana remains standing a few feet away listening intently. The little boy wriggles out of her arms and begins to kick a rubber ball around the yard.

Without interrupting the discussion, Mrs. Tiwari brings a tray with three glasses of chai, which she serves to Dick, Mr. Tiwari, and me. Then she disappears back into the house.

"Gandhi said to invest in the villages and make them productive," says Mr. Tiwari. "But . . ." His line of reasoning is interrupted as the ball rolls under his chair and the little boy crawls under to retrieve it. Then the boy gets up and says something to Mr. Tiwari in Hindi. Mr. Tiwari nods and smiles. "Poonam wants to know whether you will see tigers before you leave Sawai Modhopur."

Pryana comes over and sits in the chair beside me. "You must visit the Ranthambore tiger preserve tomorrow. If you take the early morning tour, you will be back in time to visit the press office and go to the Internet cafe in the afternoon. Then you must stay another night with us."

"Yes," agrees Mr. Tiwari. "No one comes to our city without visiting Ranthombore. It is one of the world's finest wildlife preserves."

"Oh, thank you so much," I say. "That would be great!" I had read about the tiger preserve in the guidebook. From the road today we had spotted large brown summer deer grazing in the mustard fields. I wondered whether they might have strayed from the wildlife preserve nearby.

While we are firming up plans to visit the tiger preserve, Venita, Kamlesh's oldest sister comes out and places a small plastic table between Dick and me. "My mother will bring you dinner now," she says. She goes back in and comes out with two empty plates and one plate of chapatis. Mrs. Tiwari brings a dish of something that looks like finely chopped spinach and places it on the table beside the chapatis. The spinach dish has a soupspoon sized serving utensil, but there are no forks. I remember that I have forgotten until now to instruct Dick on the proper eating custom, so I try to do it now as subtly as possible. When he starts to make a burrito, I say, "No, look," and tear of a piece of chapati into the shape of a little bird beak with which I grasp a bite sized clump of spinach. "Like this," I say.

Dick blinks at me in confusion but follows my lead. "We are trying to learn Indian customs," I explain to the family who seems to be watching us with mild amusement. I wonder when and where *they* will eat. For now at least, they are only watching. This must be another custom. Guests are served separately from the family. For me this is not a comfortable custom. I remember the nuns in school teaching us that one must never take the first bite until after the hostess lifts her fork. I think of the exuberant, jolly free-for-all of Unitarian Church potlucks at home in Seattle. It would be lots more fun for us all to eat together. Nevertheless, I cannot help but enjoy the food. The spinach dish is the most delectable version of that vegetable that I have ever tasted, flavored with a delicate blend of spices. So when Mrs. Tiwari comes out again, I say, "*Kana bota acha hai!*"

Mrs. Tiwari beams with satisfaction, bows, and says something to Pryana.

Pryana says, "Venita made the chapatis." As if on cue, Venita comes out with another plate of chapatis and a bowl of rice.

Mr. Tiwari says, "Venita cooks very well. She is engaged to be married in February."

Dick and I congratulate Venita and ask about the fiancée, how long she has known him, how they met, and so on. This switches the conversation into another gear. Venita and Rekhe take the two remaining chairs and join in.

"The parents have to find a mate for each daughter and arrange the marriage," explains Pryana. "There needs to be a dowry."

"It can be quite expensive," says Mr. Tiwari who earns the family's living by working a night shift as a nurse in a hospital.

"How expensive?" asks Dick.

"The equivalent of around $8,000," says Mr. Tiwari.

I gasp. That is a lot of money in a country where the average income amounts to only a few hundred dollars per year. "But you have three daughters," I observe. Even though the family seems comfortably middle class, I assume this to be a heavy burden.

"Dowries will consume most of my life savings," admits Mr. Tiwari. "The rest will be spent on ring ceremonies and weddings." Everyone but me laughs at this statement, made in a good-natured tone. But to me it is not funny. I decide not to make the mistake as I had with Senjeev of inviting Mr. Tiwari to visit us in America.

During the conversation, Mrs. Tiwari's solid presence comes and goes, bringing more and more food. Draped in a soft, light green flowered sari, she seems imperturbable as the Buddha. I'm not sure when it is socially acceptable to decline another helping, so I am positively stuffed before finally insisting that I cannot eat another bite. I feel immensely relieved when Mrs. Tiwari sits down on the one remaining empty chair. The little boy is gone now, having slipped out sometime during the meal and conversation. It is getting dark and the air is cooling.

Mr. Tiwari says, "Soon it will be time for me to go to the hospital. But it is our custom to gather for a short meditation at this time. Will you join us?"

"Yes, that sounds great," Dick and I nod enthusiastically. We would not miss an opportunity to partake of their life and culture.

We follow the Tiwari's inside to a small sitting room where Rekhe and Venita already sit yoga style waiting expectantly. The room is dark except for the fading light from the doorway. The walls are hung with several of Pryana's beautiful stylized paintings in stark vivid shapes and colors. One painting is of a goddess with flowing robes and veils. There is another striking rendition of a tiger with soft fur and penetrating eyes that seem both gentle and sad. One wall is lined with shelves displaying trophies, placards, and figurines, all awards the four Tiwari children had earned in schooling over the years.

Mrs. Tiwari comes in with a lighted candle and places it the center of the floor. It seems amazingly bright in the dark quiet room flickering on the marble tile flooring and illuminating the eyes now closing in soft relaxation.

"Please, sit," instructs Mr. Tiwari, assuming a perfect lotus posture on the floor.

Dick follows suit with the others on the floor, but I sit in a couch along the wall. I like to sit on the floor but usually end up more in the shape of a gangly preying mantis than a flower.

By way of instruction, Mr. Tiwari interjects only a few simple words. "Please close your eyes," he says. "Breathe in slowly filling the lungs. Breathe out slowly." Then after a pause he adds, "Picture a divine light growing within you." After that he says no more.

It doesn't take long to get into it. Sitting in the quiet darkness, I take refuge from the noisy confusion of our India adventures. Slowly inhaling the thick, warm air, I can hear other people breathing, the rubbing of cloth on floor as someone moves slightly, the faint rasp of a woman's voice from somewhere, perhaps from out in the street. And without even imagining, I can see a light. Maybe it's candlelight still present on my eyelids from when they were open or perhaps shining through them at this moment. I imagine the light growing brighter, expanding, filling not only my self but also the vastness of space beyond our galaxy and out across the Universe. In imagination at least, I have nearly reached nirvana by the time Mr. Tiwari says to open our eyes again.

Pryana switches on the electric wall light, and Mr. Tiwari leaves for work. Mrs. Tiwari comes in and sits down on the edge of a twin bed facing us across the room. Venita enters carrying a large volume under her arm. "My photo album," she says. Recalling my difficulty last night trying to think of worthy topics for Lacshmi and her friends, I am delighted that this young woman has come to the rescue with a promising conversation piece. "Great!" I exclaim. "Let's see your album."

Venita sits next to me on the couch and proceeds like a tour guide to show us through the book. There are many large glossy photos of women in identical saris made of a soft, filmy blue fabric recalling a summer sky. These dresses could easily rival ball gowns or bridesmaid's apparel in America. "Our school uniforms," announces Venita.

Still relaxed in his lotus position on the floor, Dick peers with raised eyebrow over Venita's lap into the book. "You wear those dresses every day to school?" he marvels. Venita nods and points to one of the many beautiful faces peering out from under their veils. "Here I am," she says.

The next page is filled with more shiny photos featuring several rows of resplendent female youth, all wearing sleek identical saris, but these dresses are a verdant shade of forest green with gold trim and more gold threads woven through in brocade-like patterns. "Our choir performance," declares Venita and points to one of the faces above the gowns. "Here I am," she says.

"Amazing!" I say, recalling, by contrast, the pathetic navy blue gabardine jumpers and white blouses we wore to shreds in Catholic school back in the 1950's. By senior year, the backs of our skirts were shiny and wrinkled from rubbing our bottoms against varnished wooden desk chairs. Since then most girls' schools in America have closed to make way for coeducational establishments full of their motley array of blue jeans, capri pants, sweatshirts, and ski jackets. "You have a rich and beautiful culture in India," I observe.

The next several pages contain shots of Pryana in various colorful, flowing costumes performing solo dance routines. Now there are several pages of Rekhe playing sundry roles in school plays. One photo finds her dressed as a man with a stylized curly mustache and gesturing melodramatically. This also brings back memories of high school days when I was selected to play comical male roles in plays like Chekov's *The Marriage Proposal*, or Shakespeare's *A Midsummer*

Night's Dream, because there were no boys available. If that had not been so long ago and far away, perhaps I might have recalled these memories last night in Malarna Dunger when I was struggling to think of activities Lacshmi and her friends might enjoy. Maybe they are into singing, acting, and dancing.

Mrs. Tiwari sits beaming with silent pride at this display of her daughters' talents. She is a woman perhaps younger than I am. I wonder whether she ever had the opportunity to sing, dance, and perform in school plays. But more than likely, as in the case of my own mother, she probably came out of childhood with highly creative domestic skills but with the idea of performing before an audience having never come up. Maybe we are looking at generation lag within cultures rather than at real cultural differences. Maybe, like my own daughter, Dana, Mrs. Tiwari's granddaughters will come out of school with high tech skills to earn their living in computer science and biochemistry. My theatrical skills armed me with a useful stage presence for approaching a competitive world but otherwise did not help much to earn my living.

But Venita turns the page again, "Ring ceremony!" she announces triumphantly, introducing us to scenes of vast cultural difference. Venita's perfect oval face is framed in the scallops of a sheer white veil next to a round, affable visage of male dependability exceeding the wildest expectations of his tender years. If you had to pick from a lineup of strangers one person in whom to trust the fate of your precious child, this would be your man. Below the pair of happy faces lies a satin brocade pillow upon which rests two jeweled rings. Several successive pages are filled with pictures of the couple surrounded by candles, lamps, and smiling relatives. Decked in a silken sari woven with a delicate golden pattern, Mrs. Tiwari sits slightly off center in many of the photos, glowing with love and pride.

I recall my own first engagement ceremony, such as it was. My first husband, Frank, and I had taken a semester off of graduate school to travel in *Europe on Five Dollars a Day* for two. Frank had read in the Michelin guidebook that gold was cheaper in England, so we had stopped in a little shop near the Canterbury Cathedral to buy our wedding rings. My fingers were very thin and the joints relatively large so it was hard to take it off. In fact, after he put the ring on my finger during the wedding, I did not take it off again for many years. Finally, it had to be cut off when my hand was later injured in a fall. I have never worn a ring since. In fact, for my second marriage to Dick at age fifty, the subject of rings never came up.

Maybe in these ring ceremony photos, we are viewing the surface of deep cultural differences. Marriage serves very different purposes and is far more important in India than in America. In fact, it has taken me until this very moment to grasp that purpose.

I had tried in vain to understand it from Indian novels like *The God of Small Things* by Arundati Roy and *The Death of Vishnu* by Manil Suri. Husbands and wives in these stories have very little access to one another's thoughts and feelings. They don't even seem to know one another very well and, in fact, spend most of their time with members of their own sex, not with the marriage partner. Mention is made of how infrequent the couples have sex. So I was left to wonder why they even bothered to be married. If there is no relationship and no sex, what's the point? But now, viewing Venita's ring ceremony and the joy in her mother's eyes, I realize that marriage in India provides a woman with an honored place in society, or more importantly, in that cherished unit of society known as the family. Family is what gives meaning to life. No wonder the price is high.

As Venita closes her photo album, Dick says, "If you were in a choir you must know some songs. Will you sing a song for us?"

Rekhe says, "Yes, Venita sings well. She must sing for you."

To our surprise, Venita barely hesitates. "Mmm. What shall I sing? O yes, I know a beautiful love song. It is in Hindi. It is about a woman singing in the moonlight to her lover who is far away, sitting under the same moon." She starts to sing in a crystal clear soprano voice a lilting melody enhanced with the whining exotic fluctuations characteristic of Indian and Middle Eastern music. As she finishes, everyone cheers and Mrs. Tiwari beams with pride.

Before the applause has yet subsided, Rekhe says, "Now Pryana must dance. This suggestion elicits a round of discussion in Hindi between mother and daughters during which Pryana and Rekhe leave the room momentarily. Rekhe comes back with a small tape player and a stack of cassettes. She sits down on the floor and begins to sort through the tapes. "It's okay for Pryana to dance. Pappa isn't here. This dancing would embarrass him."

Dick raises his eyebrow. "It must be pretty good then," he says.

Rekhe slips the tape into the machine, which emits popular Indian music, wailing wind instruments and a background of steady drumbeats. We are enjoying the music almost to the point of wanting to dance ourselves when Pryana swirls into the room. She is barefoot and clothed in a jumpsuit of white silk with blue flowers. The outfit is very modest with long sleeves and long pant legs, tightened only at the wrists and ankles. Her slender waist is banded with a wide blue satin ribbon. She dances with a blue satin *dupatta* which she waves about, weaving it in and out of her arms. Her choreography seems to be an eclectic composite of disco, modern interpretive, and traditional belly dancing. Soon she discards the dupatta and, thus unencumbered, pours body and soul into rhythm and movement. As the music stops, Pryana bows to cheers and applause. Mrs. Tiwari again beams with pride.

Rekhe says, "Now Mona must sing a song from America."

"Mona sings in our church choir," says Dick.

My first thought is to flatly refuse. Pryana would be a hard act to follow. But, on the other hand, it would be fun, given a few disclaimers. "Sure I sing in choir, but I have never performed a solo in public."

"This is not in public. It is here at home with us," Venita points out. "If you sing in a choir, you must know many songs."

It's true. I know many songs, but not from our church choir wherein I sing tenor and almost never the melody. The ones I recall are camp songs, long trapped in the chambers of childhood memory. The one escaping now is "The Ash Grove," probably dredged up because of its similarity to Venita's melancholy, lilting melody.

As I start to sing, Mrs. Tiwari gives me a withering look of disapproval, or so I imagine. Maybe in India it's inappropriate for a grandmotherly type with my limited talent to take this on. But, as Venita says, "This is not in public."

CHAPTER 10

A Voice from Home

We are pressing deeper into rural India. Almost no one speaks English. When I hand curious on-lookers a Hindi newspaper article to read about us, they wobble their heads as if to imply that they can't read at all. Pushing the bike and wending our way through the crowds of one village this morning, we had to go around the carcass of a huge gray buffalo, its big horns curling up to eye level, flies crawling in and out of its enormous nostrils. Later, pedaling away from another village, we passed the half-eaten body of a razor-back pig. No wonder Indians are, like Dick and me, mostly vegetarian. Who would have any appetite for meat after watching stray scavenger dogs cleaning up on whatever happens to die in the street?

It has been two days since we have seen a boiled egg wallah. That means no protein. Around midmorning, I spotted a man with steam pouring out of a big kettle. Surrounded by the mob, I made my way up to him, hoping to buy some eggs. Instead he had little blobs of something frying in a big pool of grease. So we had blobs of fried dough for lunch. Having found no banana wallah this morning, I bought an apple, but I am unwilling to spare enough of my drinking water to wash it.

What a joke on ourselves! In planning this trip, I suppose we had imagined stopping at restaurants for lunch, going inside, and peacefully eating some delectable little Indian dish one might order in Seattle or, better still, like the Mrs. Tiwaris might serve. But even when we do find a restaurant, it is usually outdoors and has a metal roof held up with rough cut poles over a dirt floor. The food would be good, but we would be totally mobbed the whole time we were eating. If we did find an indoor restaurant (original concept), what would we do with the bike? Even if we locked it to a tree, the bike would be the one mobbed and likely stripped of various souvenirs, a pedal, a bell, a gear shift lever. By the time we came out, our precious vehicle might very well be totaled. So we shop in market stalls and eat beside the road as far as possible from town. Even there, eating is a strange experience as locals gather round to stare while we munch. Sometimes we try to converse with them, but other times we just let them watch us in silence. But we always bow and say, "Namaste," before mounting up to ride away.

Such is the real rural India. It's a good thing we stayed behind the extra day in Sawai Modophur to see Rhathanbore National Park. That was almost like visiting the imaginary India left over from childhood memories of illustrated Rudyard Kipling storybooks. A white sun sphere penetrated the gray fog of this *Jungle Book,* a sprawling lattice work of branches through which long-armed, gray langur apes performed amazing gymnastic feats. Green parrots perched about on branches like shiny ornaments. Slender white egrets spread graceful wings to float effortlessly over golden undergrowth heavily populated with deer, their orange velveteen coats aglow with radiant polka dots. We did not see any tigers in Ranthambore which, from the *Jungle Book* point of view, would have been a plus. As I recall, Shere Khan, the tiger, was quite the villain of the story. What we saw, instead, was an abundant supply of food for that now-endangered species of cat, once hated and relentlessly hunted.

The most intrusive reality on that unusually cold morning was the large open-air canter in which we were hurled along gravel roads, stirring up a cold, dusty wind. Having been comfortably warm since our arrival in India, we had not anticipated such a cold, foggy morning, so clothed in a single layer of thin nylon, I shivered the whole way. Every so often, the canter would stop, and a dozen tourists, the

We pause beside the road in open country.

only westerners we've seen since Agra, would stand up in front of us
and begin snapping photos of wild boar or blue antelope grazing on
dry yellow grass beside the road. I returned from Ranthambore with
a bad cold which seems mostly gone now after bicycling several
days in warm sunshine, but my nose and throat are still irritated by
something in the air.

We pedal up through the village of Indargarh with its temple
spires and ancient walled city climbing the hillside. We have passed
quite a few hills in the last few days and have even had to pedal over
some reasonably challenging ones, pulling our heavy trailer. But in

most cases, the roads in this part of India pass between the mountains, giving us grand views of their spires and camel humps which must have inspired the interesting architecture of Hindu temples.

Last night we stayed in the town of Lakheri in a fairly decent hotel. Our room had a window looking out over the town and the cement factory with its smoke stack reaching for the sky as if in height competition with the surrounding hills. One of the windowpanes was missing, so we plugged it with the curtain to keep out the cold smoky air. Nothing is perfect after all.

We pass what looks like another encampment of nomads. People sit around fires or under tents haphazardly constructed of poles with burlap bags for walls and grass for roofs. A rush of adrenaline multiplies the pedal power in my legs as I unintentionally make eye contact with a teenaged boy standing among a group of his pals. He gives out a yelp like an excited jackal and takes out after us followed by the rest of his pack, all hooting, hollering, and panting like they're about to corner a rabbit. From now on this trusty tandem will be known as *blue rabbit* for the way she leaves those boys in the dust. Looking back, I can see them giving up and turning back to their camp.

Crossing a railroad track, I spot a chai wallah and call out for Dick to stop. If the fellow has chai, he may at least have some boiled water to wash my apple. I dismount, run up to the counter and call out, "Pani? Boiled?"

The chai wallah wobbles his head from side to side. Then he lifts a bucket out from under the counter and removes a stainless steel lid. Peering in I note that the bucket is full of what looks like clean water with a copper dipping vase floating on top.

"Boiled?" I ask.

The chai wallah wobbles his head again. "Drinking water," he assures me with complete confidence. At this moment, I make a crucial decision to forever break the rules, to forego all the warnings and prophesies of doom. I am tired of going thirsty for days on end while hunting in vain for water that fulfills Joan's stringent requirement of being bottled. If it's drinking water for the beautiful people of India, it's drinking water for Dick and me. So I use the copper vase to fill my water bottle and wash my apple. "Thank you very much," I say. Then I bow and say, "Namaste."

The chai vendor bows and bestows upon me a smile of profound satisfaction as though helping me out has made his day.

We cross a train track and turn onto a major arterial leading to the town of Kota, which the guidebook describes as an ancient city founded in 1264 following some tribal warfare. In the 17th century, the city reportedly enjoyed prominence as a palace headquarters of the Mughal Emperor, Jehangir. Today, according to *Lonely Planet Guide to India*, "It has the dubious honor of being Rajasthan's industrial center (mainly for chemicals.)" It is reported to have a sizable market area and a couple of decent hotels, so our plan is to lay over there for a day or two and solve all our earthly problems. Maybe we will find an Internet café and an STD phone stand so Dick can bug Bike Friday again about sending the inner tubes to Chennai. If the Kota market proves versatile, maybe I can find another tan sweater to replace the one that mysteriously disappeared from the bike's luggage rack yesterday. I also hope to buy a pair of flip-flops with which to wade through dirty bathroom puddles in the middle of the night. Most of all I entertain the faint hope of meeting in Kota my first drug store wallah who knows about dental floss.

As we draw nearer to Kota, we encounter our first total traffic jam with a morass of cars stopped dead as on a Seattle freeway during rush hour. So we get off and push the bike along the rocky shoulder, pursued by our usual mob of fans. At the edge of town, the road crosses the wide Chambal River. Rising up from the opposite shore is a vertical cliff topped with a variable array of cement block houses. The road is lined on either side with the blackest, most dismal display of vendor stalls we have ever seen. Most of these small business establishments specialize in some kind of greasy hardware, engine parts, scrap metal, sewer pipe, slabs of rock, bricks, concrete block and the like. Every inch of everything is covered with layers of gray dust, and film. The air is thick with soot. I had long since abandoned my eternal search for the egg wallah, when suddenly there he is along with a number of other food stalls tucked in amongst this most unappetizing array of industrial filth. There stands his big kettle of boiling water, its cloud of steam rising above scrap metal roofing hung with makeshift Hindi signage. It is hard to imagine food served in this setting, but I suppose even dirty, used hardware vendors have to eat.

By the time I have replenished our supply of eggs, bananas, and samosas, the traffic has started to move again, so we mount up. The clogged arterial soon empties into a big traffic circle from which an explosion of motorcycles, auto rickshaws, buses, trucks and camel carts erupt like the grand finale at a fireworks display. But we had been forewarned. Given its usual penchant for understatement, the guidebook describes Kota as, "noisy and plagued with traffic." We edge our way to a traffic policeman who stands alongside the circle, making sporadic futile attempts to order the chaos. "*Hotel kaha hai?*" Dick calls out. The officer nods and points us onto the main thoroughfare. Although it is still fairly early in the day, our plan is to find a hotel, lock the bike inside, and complete our errands on foot or by taxi. Bicycling under these conditions is not our idea of fun.

* * * *

Walking from our hotel toward the market, we cross the artificial lake of Kishore Sagar built in 1346. Like most bodies of water we have seen in India, this lake is covered with a frothy sheen afloat with plastic bags, aluminum cans, and sundry debris. Although it is a fairly large lake, only one craft is in view, a small rickety rowboat sans oars. Its passenger crew consists of two small boys who dangle their hands in the dirty water and paw about as if feeling for something underneath. Away off in the distance we spot a small island crowned with an eighteenth century yellow stone palace of some long defeated Moghul emperor. This image of children playing, or probably struggling somehow for survival, amidst contemporary industrial pollution in the shadow of vanished wealth seems to sum up India, or perhaps even the entire modern world, in one panoramic view.

On the opposite side of the street and even along the lakeshore itself, market stalls abound. In fact, as far as we can tell, just about every street in Kota is lined with vending stalls. We turn away from the lake and enter a narrow market street that seems to go on forever into the distance. Each time we come to a cross street, that too leads off into an endless line of market stalls. Our guest house manager in Bombay had said, "Virtually anything can be bought in India." Perhaps that's true, but unless you were born and raised in a town and had been shopping there all your life, how would you find this *anything*?

Milling through the crowds in narrow Kota streets, buzzed and beeped by motorcycles and rickshaws, I realize that this must truly be the place where almost *anything* can be bought — well, maybe not dental floss. This seems to be more like Home Depot than Walgreens. There are vendor stalls with stacks upon stacks of those big metal bowls women sit beside on the floor to wash dishes or balance on their heads to haul everything from laundry to firewood. There are the pottery jugs with which children carry water from irrigation ditches to their huts for washing and doing laundry. There are pots and pans, kitchen utensils, slabs of rock, floor tiles. Most interesting are the fabric merchants with hundreds of exquisite designs. Most pieces are carefully folded and piled on shelves but many hang along the streets like colorful banners exposed to dust and air pollution.

We stop at a shoe store and buy a pair of flip-flops for 28 rupees, the equivalent of sixty cents. Farther on we spot a large stall whose walls are hung with women's sweaters mostly adorned with intricate embroidery or beaded patterns. Dick encourages me to buy a fancy one as a souvenir of India, but I'm just looking to fill the hole in my wardrobe created by the disappearance of my simple tan cardigan which must have fallen off the bike yesterday. I need something that won't clash with my one loud bicycle jersey or two colorful T-shirts. As far as I can tell only one of the sweaters at this shop is plain and unadorned. It is a warm shade of brown without baubles or bangles. I point to it, and the vendor brings it to the counter for me to try on. Unfortunately, the sleeves barely cover my elbows and the girth isn't ample enough to button across my chest.

I shake my head and hand the sweater back. "Bigger," I insist, spreading my hands apart in an expansive gesture. The vendor brings out a number of different sweaters before I find one both big enough and plain enough for me. It is pretty much monochromatic tan except for a subtle leaf pattern machine-knitted through with fine gray, almost black, yarn. The vendor asks 500 rupees for the item, insisting that it is of very fine quality, but Dick haggles him down to 450. That's the equivalent of about ten dollars in American money and should be considered a great bargain. But it's a hefty price considering that this sweater is to replace one I had bought secondhand for three dollars at Seattle Goodwill.

We are nearing the end of a mile-long market street and will soon head up the hill for a visit to the town's major tourist attraction, the large City Palace. But I still peer intently at the merchandise in every stall hoping one will be a pharmacy. Just as a motorcycle charges by narrowly missing my right elbow, there is an explosive sound like gunfire underfoot. I can see smoke rising from my shoe. I'm not sure whether the motorcycle has blown an engine gasket or one of us has triggered a land mine. Maybe my journeys through life and India have come to an abrupt end. But peels of laughter trail off into the distance as a gang of little boys runs down the street and ducks between the stalls. I flush with humiliation but then recall my favorite Gandhi quote, "The seeker after truth must become humbler than dust. Only then and not 'til then will he have a glimpse of truth." Any humble truth seeker would take a childish firecracker prank quite literally in stride. Feeling genuinely amused, I smile to myself as we start up hill toward the palace.

Arriving at the entrance, we are informed that the palace is closed on Fridays. So we have to content ourselves with a stroll, arm in arm, about the perimeter of this huge complex, gazing up at its many fluted Moslem window frames and golden onion domes, the team of giant elephant statues supporting its arched entry way. Looking back in the direction from which we have come, it is easy to imagine the Emperor Jehangir ascending the wide cobblestone street with his elephants and fanfare, accompanied by an entourage of courtiers draped in splendid golden robes and red turbans.

But even here, today's real India intrudes upon that vision of bygone splendor. What must have once been a magnificent palace courtyard now looks more like the parking lot of a low-end shopping mall, sparsely surfaced with fine black gravel, cinders perhaps from a factory coal furnace. Beneath a grand arched portal sits the rusty hulk of an old Volkswagen bus. A patch of thirsty weeds growing from its hood attests to the incalculable duration of the car's abandonment. Healthier crops of weeds protrude from beyond the palace outer walls that keep the neighborhood pigs and cows at bay. The back of the palace commands a view over a large dam and out across the lake. A roadway, heavy with traffic, crosses the dam toward huge billowing smoke stacks and a motley collection of tumble-down buildings on the other side of town.

* * * *

We are back at the hotel before we finally stumble upon a drugstore to ask about dental floss. Tucked in under the eaves of our hotel, this stall is quite the largest and best-stocked pharmacy I have yet seen. A slender three-foot fluorescent bulb illuminates orderly shelves of glimmering bottles and jars with glitzy labels. A bespectacled young gentleman at the counter greets me in English as I approach. "Good evening, Madame," he says. "May I help you?" This is promising.

"Do you have dental floss?" I ask, my fingers poised to pantomime if necessary.

"No!" His head makes a perpendicular side to side swivel, no dubious wobble.

"Do you know where I can buy dental floss?"

"Not in India."

"Why?"

"Factory in Bangalore close down one and a half years."

"No! You mean they stopped making dental floss. Why?"

"Factory close. No one make dental floss."

"Couldn't they import it from another country?" I suggest.

He shrugs. "No one buy dental floss."

"You mean no one wants it?"

"No . . . one . . . buy . . . dental . . . floss," he repeats, emphasizing every word as if speaking to a child with a developmental disability.

My jaw drops. My heart skips several beats. Six more weeks without dental floss is unthinkable. Going without a bath or shower is a nothing. Washing out snotty handkerchiefs in cold water is not a problem. But sitting in dingy hotel rooms fumbling in the dark to floss my teeth with a piece of thread from Dick's emergency sewing kit is intolerable. The thread keeps breaking. I have to take a new piece and start all over several times before I'm finished.

For the past several decades, flossing has been the most essential part of my indomitable bathroom ritual, so great is my fear of losing my teeth! My father and both paternal aunts had false teeth long before they were my age. I have seen their miserable grimaces as they felt about with their tongues to remove food caught between their dentures and their gums. Because conditions like this tend to be hereditary, I resolved long ago to floss and gum brush religiously. So far it has worked. I have many crowns over filled and refilled teeth that have fallen apart, but every capped and multiple-filled incisor is still firmly rooted in healthy gums. But who knows how much periodontal deterioration might accrue from several more floss-less weeks?

"Maybe you'll have to use toothpicks, " Dick suggests. Since we ran out of dental floss, I have seen poor, patient Dick at night running picks carefully along the edge of his gums, but I have no faith in the method.

"Yes. Toothpicks." The drug store wallah nods several times in rapid secession. He retrieves a small box of them from one of the shelves and plops it on the counter in front of me.

I will not be consoled. "No dental floss in India! How can you live without dental floss? Don't your teeth rot and fall out of your mouth?"

"Yes!" he says.

I know from the way he said, "Yes!" that the conversation is over. There could be no arguing with such absolutism, and besides, I have evidenced the truth of his claim in the dark gaping caverns of people's mouths.

But something about the way he says, "Yes," seems to imply a lot more. It says I should get a grip. Permanently losing teeth by the time you're my age, that is if you happen to be lucky enough to live that long, is as natural as growing them was in infancy or losing your baby teeth at age six and growing them again. The appearance of a full set of pearly whites when I smile is quite illusory.

I once asked my dentist for an inventory. My four first bicuspids were removed for orthodontia in my teens. Later all four wisdom teeth were dug out in surgery. Another third of my teeth have crowns. That leaves only about one third of the originals, all of which are multiply filled. If it weren't for thousands of dollars paid by the Washington State Employees dental health plan, I would be toothless.

Changing the subject, I ask the man, "Is there an STD phone near by?"

"Around the corner," he says.

"Are you going to make a phone call?" Dick asks.

"We have to call Bike Friday in Eugene and bug them again about the inner tubes," I remind him.

Dick says, "It's five AM in Oregon. The stores aren't open yet."

"It's eight in Boston," I say.

"Oh, you're going to call Dana. That's a good idea," says Dick. "Give her my love."

"Yes, I'll give her our love and ask her to send some dental floss to the Palm Grove Hotel in Chennai."

* * * *

I stand at the counter in front of the STD stall trying to plug my right ear with my finger while I pick up the receiver from the STD machine and hold it up to my left ear. But I have to unplug my right ear to dial in the number. I carefully enter the country code, the area code and then the familiar number. Because of the noise in the street, I can just barely hear the phone ringing enough to realize with relief that the connection was made. The attendant sees me plugging my ear again, so he takes pity on me and gestures to me to come and sit inside the stall. There the acoustics are a little better but far from perfect.

"Hello, this is Dana," says a faint but wonderfully familiar voice into my left ear. The sound of my own dear daughter's voice is like angels singing in heaven. There is so much caring in it, so much comfort. Hearing the voice of this person I miss so much overwhelms me with a powerful awareness of how much I miss all the comforts and easiness of my life in America. The homesickness previously gnawing at the edges of my soul now moves in and takes over.

From time to time on this trip, I have thought about the comforts of home and felt guilty for missing them. I have felt positively remorseful about how good it will feel to go back to a home big enough to afford me a space to have my own office with my own computer and a big window looking out across town at Mount Rainier projected like an apparition upon a screen of hazy sky. It seems criminal that I will go back there and leave an old woman I chanced to see in Bombay outside her hovel of crates and tin roofing. If all humans are created equal, the economic justice equation is way out of balance.

"Dana, it's Mom."

"Mom! Oh, Mom, I'm so glad you called. I've been worried, wondering how you're doing."

It's true that I don't get to see Dana very much when I'm in the States, what with her living in Boston, but missing her is a pain I endure every moment of my life even as I now miss home. The one pain of loss brings to mind the other. But this time I manage to ward off the accompanying guilt and wallow in my homesickness without a trace of remorse.

"I'm doing pretty well. I have a cough. My nose runs a lot."

"Do you have a cold?"

"No. I think it's the air."

"You never had allergies before."

"There's always a first time."

"Are you having a good time? How's India?"

"India is amazing!"

"I bet. What the most amazing thing?"

"Everything."

"For example?"

There are more camel carts on the road than cars.

"There are more camel carts on the road than cars."

"That's pretty amazing. Where are you calling from?"

"An STD stand in Kota," I say but then realize that answer communicates nothing. So I go on to explain that Kota is more than half way between Agra and Ujjain where we will catch a train for our side trip to the meeting in Chennai. I describe the STD stand in detail, the tiny hole in the wall, a sort of three-sided room with a photo copy machine that you can pay to use and the little cash register phone gadget on the counter. I describe the beautiful little shrine in the corner with its statue of Shiva, its garland of flowers, its copper incense burner. "As far as I can tell there are few stores in India as we know them, just these little three sided stalls. This one happens to be a print shop and pay phone business."

"That's truly amazing," she says. "What an experience you must be having!"

With that, the homesick spirit vacates my soul again, and the spirit of adventure moves back in. After all, tonight I will sleep in a reasonably clean hotel. There is even an indoor restaurant where Dick and I will sit together at a private table and eat dinner, admittedly without forks. "Yes, this is the experience of a lifetime. Everyone in America should spend time in India. Then they will be educated."

"Yes, we are so spoiled here in America."

Reflecting upon the deeper implications of that comment brings back the serious business of my call. "Speaking of spoiled, I was wondering whether you might be able to send some dental floss to the Palm Grove Hotel in Chennai."

"Yes, I'd be happy to, Mom. Is there anything else you need?"

I think about that a moment. There are lots of things I need. "Yes, I need some wet wipes."

"Wet wipes?"

"You know, baby wipes."

"Oh? What for?"

Rather than going into gory details about colitis attacks and rudimentary bathroom facilities, I say, "For keeping clean. Often there is no soap and water."

"Okay. What else?"

I think again. "Ludens Wild Cherry Menthol Cough Drops."

"How many of each of these things do you want?"

"Lots."

"Three packs?"

"Yes, three large packs."

"When will you arrive in Chennai?"

"December twenty-fifth."

"Christmas! This will be my Christmas present to you, Mom. I'm so glad you phoned to tell me what you want for Christmas. I will be your Santa."

"I hope the stuff arrives in time. We'll only be there a few days."

"The package will arrive by Christmas," she says with complete confidence. "I'll send it by Airborne Express. By regular mail, it would take a couple of months. You would be back by then." My daughter's competence has always astounded me. Ever since the age of four, she has managed to come up with the right solution, to know exactly what to do and how to do it. Even so, she has always been sweet, helpful, and unassuming. It is not surprising that she holds down a management job with a large biotechnology firm.

"That will be pretty expensive," I say. I recall once pricing the shipping cost of Airborne Express for a gift that needed to arrive overseas in time for a wedding. The amount was many times the value of the item, so I had given up on the idea and sent it late by surface mail.

"Sure Mom, but you're worth it. I love you."

After we say our goodbyes and hang up, I remember something else. I should have asked for Kleenex. Oh well, I can swipe some napkins from the hotel restaurant.

CHAPTER 11

The Road from Hell

We are now three days out of Kota.

Before we left Kota, Dick had promised that we would be traveling on *The Main Highway.* The phrase had conjured up images of a cross between a U.S. interstate and a major Bombay thoroughfare, in short, certain death. In fact, the first few miles had indeed been almost that scary, but the farther we got away from the city center, the calmer I felt. An incessant cacophony of horns screeched and trumpeted around us, but I took a modicum of comfort in the sight of vendors with wares laid out along the roadside and pedestrians meandering ahead of us. If these brave souls expected to live until sunset, so might we.

After we were well out of town, I began to realize that in India *The Main Highway* is much like any secondary road except that the pavement is a little wider and firmer. Bicycling was actually easier. We passed a similar assortment of goatherds and ox carts. A comparable variety of buses and colorfully painted trucks charged around us. What changed most was the landscape. There was an eerie feeling about it. Cattle nibbled at the few blades of grass cropping up sporadically across a wasteland of mudflats that gradually gave way to a limitless expanse of flat dry land. Pedestrians and cows were fewer and farther between. This was the greatest expanse of empty, unpopulated acreage we had yet seen in India. The desolate scene was shrouded by a thick haze through which the sun was visible but cast no shadow.

Whereas on secondary roads we had passed mostly productive farmland, on *The Main Highway* we began to see industrial sights set back from the road. A large A-frame structure displayed a sign that read, "Consolidated Proteins, LLD." Another big box edifice featured piles of a white powdery substance that looked like lime. Women in saris strode gracefully as models on a runway up and down the mounds carrying bowls of the limestone on their heads.

Much of the second day we skimmed along through a flat plain stretching away for miles on either side, all brown and sparsely vegetated like a cross between Kansas and Eastern Washington. It was smooth sailing and stressless until we spotted a big transport truck overturned on its side adjacent to the roadway. Three men sat beside the truck looking helpless and forlorn. We looked back at them as we cruised by, but couldn't think of any way to help. Since then, I have felt a little more anxious whenever a horn blasts from behind warning of a truck roaring by. I would not want to be under the thing if it overturned.

By now, on the third day out of Kota toward Ujjain, road conditions have taken a turn for the worse. We have dubbed this *the road from hell*. The Highway Department has been busy grating off the entire layer of blacktop to replace it with new pavement. We are cycling over a bed of sharp stones the size of softballs. We had previously encountered short stretches of unpaved roadbed like this, especially inside villages. Under such conditions, we normally get off and walk the bike until the pavement resumes. But we cannot out-walk this. It has been this way ever since early morning. Scarcely breathing, we pedal in slow motion for fear of another flat tire.

Crawling up over the crest of a hill, we confront the road crew. It is a group of women in saris. One shovels rocks into large metal bowls. The others march out into the roadway carrying the bowls on their heads and dump the rocks into the dust, which billows up around them. The colors of their saris are barely discernible beneath the coating of gray dust. I gape in disbelief. It feels uncomfortable enough to bicycle with road dirt caked on my skin, clogging my cuticles, and smeared across the front of my bicycle jersey. How would it be to haul rock out here in something resembling an evening gown?

A man driving a new Japanese car stops and gets out to talk with us. "Road very bad," he says.

"Yes, very bad," Dick agrees.

"Twelve more kilometers road bad. Then Madya Pradesh. Road good," he reassures us. By that, I figure he means the road construction will go on for twelve more kilometers until we reach the state line. We take heart to know there is an end to this, but even so, twelve more kilometers is a long way at the rate we're going.

* * * *

By late afternoon, we have stopped to fix two more flat tires and have made two side-trips up more unpaved roads through villages in a fruitless quest for staples. So we are still in the road construction zone. In fact, I'm beginning to wonder if these conditions will exist all the way to Ujjain. As for now, it's getting late and we begin to search for lodging.

I spot what must be a mirage. In contrast with the industrial sites and ramshackle huts we have passed all day, this structure seems positively unreal, like an illustration from a children's poetry anthology. Set back from the roadway is a cluster of modern buildings with true straight lines and clean new paint. Off to one side is a small cube of a building constructed with precision and painted a soft sunny yellow. A pair of varnished wooden doors opens in front and a pink balustrade crowns the roof. The sign in front reads, "Guest House," in plain English.

"Look. Guest House," I call out to Dick.

I stand with the bike at the end of the driveway while Dick goes to inquire. I can see him gesturing and talking with two men. He goes inside with them. When they come back out, Dick motions for me to come forward. "I think they're saying the Guest House is brand new and hasn't opened yet, but maybe we can stay here anyway," he says. "Come, look inside."

The inside of this little house is like something out of a dream.

Everything is brand new. In fact, a young workman with a broom stands in the corner sweeping up the remains of a little construction dust. Otherwise the place is spotless. The flooring is pure marble. The bathroom walls are covered with shiny white tiles in a lacy floral patterns, reminiscent of the Taj Mahal and fit for a princess. I wonder whether our dingy hotel room in Gangaphur might have looked like this before neglect took over.

"Very nice," I say, barely noticing that there is no bed, just a bare, empty floor.

"I think they said they can bring us in a cot," says Dick. That sounds credible to me. We had slept quite comfortably several nights ago on a cot made of plastic strips woven over an aluminum frame like a big lawn chair.

"That would be great!" I am ecstatic at the thought of staying in such a clean, little house.

But then, unpredictably the mood changes. The two men begin speaking Hindi together in hushed tones. One of them turns to us and says in English, "Guesthouse two kilometers, town of Susner" and points down the road. The young man grabs a rusty hulk of bicycle leaning against a tree and motions for us to follow. We obey reluctantly. So the pretty little, sparkling clean guesthouse was only a mirage after all. It will not materialize for us.

When we reach the town, the young man jumps off his bike, props it up on a rusty kickstand and runs off across the street. We can see him speaking to a middle aged man and pointing at us. But I soon lose track of him as an unruly mob swarms in around us. In fact, I can't really see anyone but Quasimodo, the hunchback of Notre Dame, standing right in front of me with snot running down his Mortimer Snurd countenance. He grabs at my arms and leaves black handprints on my pink windbreaker.

"Hotel?" I ask, even though it occurs to me that the Quasimodo guy might be developmentally disabled.

The Quasimodo guy yells something in Hindi. Everyone laughs.

"Guest house?" Dick tries again.

The people look at one another and then start shouting in rapid Hindi. A couple of them point to a building back off to the left. It is clearly the most intact structure of the town, sitting off the street behind a gated fence with a driveway curving around in front. With difficulty, we turn the bike and trailer around, maneuvering them through the crowd and on down the driveway. But when we reach the entrance to the building, we find that the doors are locked. Two men stand beside the driveway just looking at us and saying nothing while we point at the door and ask, "Guest house?" several times.

The older one walks up to us and says, "No Anglaise."

We aren't sure whether he means no one speaks English or that no English speaking guests are welcome—or both.

The younger man comes forward and says, "Booked. All rooms booked." Somehow I am suspicious. Far from full, the building seems deserted. It is hard to believe that this place is really booked, way out here in the middle of nowhere, accessible only by a roadway that has been demolished for construction. I have no idea why he would lie to us, but finer nuances of meaning and motivation are guesswork at best. We have to take everything at face value.

So here we are Mary-and-Joseph-like, with no room at the inn. A stable will not suffice even if there is one available. A few wise men and several shepherds would be insignificant compared with the number of visitors we would attract sleeping out in the open. So we fall back on our last resort. "Police thane?" I ask.

The younger man points down the road in the direction from which we have come, and we are off again carefully maneuvering the bike through the crowd. The mob moves along beside us shouting confusion in Hindi. Soon I spot a man in uniform standing beside the road watching as if with intense curiosity. "There's a policeman," I call up to Dick.

Dick edges the bike in the direction of the man in uniform.

Neither "hotel" nor "guesthouse" seems to register any meaning with the policemen. He just stares at us while the crowd shouts at him in a chaotic babble of Hindi.

Dick tries another word. "Lodging?" he asks.

This seems to register some meaning to the policeman. He nods and points to a nice looking young man at the edge of the crowd and babbles something about lodging. The young man gestures for us to follow him.

As we approach the place destined hopefully to be our *lodging* for the night, it becomes clear that the distinction between *hotel, guesthouse,* and *lodging* are not subtle. In fact the term "lodging" is closer in meaning to *hovel* than it is to *hotel.* This place makes the dismal Basant Hotel in Gangaphur look like the Ritz. The building is constructed of three concrete walls, discolored various shades of green, gray, and smoky black like army camouflage.

We enter by way of the *restaurant.* Well, anyway it serves food. This part of the building is a makeshift addition of rough-cut poles supporting a roof of corrugated scrap metal. The dirt floor oozes black dust and ashes inches thick. In the center is a four cubic feet concrete box thickly coated with black soot. This must be the stove. A hole in its side serves as ventilation. There is another hole on top. That's where the fire comes out. A blackened kettle sits on the fire. A woman wearing a dirty purple sari stands beside the fire chopping vegetables on top of the blackened concrete. A few customers sit about at a shabby collection of mismatched benches and tables, variously splattered with paint.

We climb a banisterless concrete staircase in back, walk across a roof top, and enter one bedroom through which we have to pass to reach our own. There is just barely enough space for one person to walk around our double bed. There are no other furnishings. Trying not to touch anything, I set my pack on a shelf built into the wall. When I accidentally touch the mattress pad, grease mixed with dust and soot rubs off on my fingertips. There is no electricity in the room, and darkness is rapidly approaching.

I sit down on the edge of the bed in twilight with hands folded in my lap, wondering how I will fill the empty hours until bedtime. It is six-thirty PM on December 21, the shortest day of the year. A brisk wind blows in through the window, which has an iron grating and metal shutters, but no glass. I shiver a little, but don't even feel motivated to search among the luggage for my sweater. I am immobilized by a depression of homesickness, intolerable longing for clean white sheets and hot bathtubs, trappings of privilege in a grossly inequitable world.

Dick goes out to use the toilet stall on the roof. I am not eager to try that. It too has no electricity and no window at all, just a hole in the floor and a water barrel. I will not use the water. There is no way to tell what might be lurking in its invisible depths.

Dick comes back in and invites me to go down stairs and have some dinner. I am not hungry. Maybe it was my glimpse of the cooking facilities.

Is there a light down there?" I ask.

"Yes. It's warmer down there too."

"I'll come down and watch you eat." Besides, I want to work on my diary.

* * * *

My back is to the cooking stove when the food arrives on a shiny stainless steel platter. It looks good enough to restore my appetite, especially the "green salad." There are tomatoes, carrots, horseradish, and onions, all cut into slices nearly equal in diameter. In India, this is called a "green salad" even though the only thing green on the plate is a small wedge of lime to squeeze over the top. I think by green, they mean *raw*. Joan had warned us never to eat raw vegetables in India, but I have already transgressed once or twice and eaten a *green salad* without dire consequences. I must be on the verge of scurvy the way the sight of this platter instantly restores my appetite. I devour everything on it in the twinkling of an eye, then treat myself to a little Dahl (lentils) and half a chapati.

As we finish eating, the proprietor brings his beautiful five-year-old daughter, Maya, and introduces her to us. They sit down beside us and try to converse, the father translating with his 10 words of English. The subject matter is limited to the usual, age, marital status, number of children, but in such exchanges a sense of soul and personality can still be communicated. These are beautiful, loving people with reverence for family life and curiosity about the world.

After the little girl leaves to go home for bed, I try to work on my diary, but suddenly at around eight o'clock, the lights blink out all over town. At first we wonder what to do next, but then following the lead of people at other tables, we just sit there calmly in the darkness chatting as if nothing could be more natural and common place.

Eventually a kerosene lamp comes on in the back, so I move close and continue to write in my diary. Dick says, "I'm turning in," and heads up the stairs.

I was kidding myself to think that I would be able to write in my diary. Within minutes, perhaps twenty young men have gathered around me. They gawk at me as though I am a weird sea creature in an aquarium display tank. They appear eager to get acquainted, but I notice a judgmental, sardonic expression in some of their eyes. I note that some of them are wearing Moslem caps and turbans. Some have beards. They are well-dressed in clean, satin robes or carefully pressed pants. It seems as if they have cleaned themselves up for a special evening on the town.

The conversation starts with the usual name, age, profession, and number of children. Then quite suddenly, as if out of the blue, one of them asks, "Madame, what do you think of Osama Bin Laden?"

I am beginning to suspect that there might be a political reason why we were not admitted to either of the two guesthouses in this town. After all, we are Americans. Perhaps to some of these people, we are the ENEMY, the invaders. Maybe this question is meant to trap me into saying something I shouldn't. But it is best to be honest, so I reply, "Osama Bin Laden needs to learn that violence only begets more violence. He should study the teachings of Gandhi." The young men all look at one another in confusion and surprise. Several of them sneer or snicker.

"Have the leaders of America studied Gandhi's teaching?" one of them asks.

I shrug. "Apparently not!"

"What is the book you're writing?" one of them asks.

"I'm keeping a diary. I hope to write a book about our travels in India."

"What name your book?"

"Humbler than Dust. The title is from a quote by Gandhi. *The seeker after truth must become humbler than dust. Only then and not 'till then will he ever have a glimpse of truth.*"

Even though I did not expect them to even understand the quote, the young men all nod gravely. For some mysterious reason it has won them over, and they now know I am their friend.

* * * *

Before turning in, I close the metal shutter and slip the greasy pillow into a clean T-shirt, which will serve as a pillowcase. Then I crawl into our silk travel sheet beside Dick. He is already sleeping, and his body feels warm. It is the same portable heater I take along on backpacking trips in the mountains of Washington State. I think how stupid it was of me to shudder at first sight of our *lodging*. Lying here in the darkness, I cannot see or feel the lack of cleanliness. In a few moments I will be totally unconscious and oblivious of my surroundings which, for the price of a hundred rupees, less than two dollars and fifty cents, what more could I ask?

CHAPTER 12

Ujjain

Two days after our unsavory night in Susner, Dick and I have a salubrious time making early morning love in our hotel room on the top floor of the Chandra Gupta Hotel directly across the street from the railway station in Ujjain. All the while a joyous religious chant, perhaps from a popular radio or television broadcast, blares up through the orchestral backdrop of auto horns and engine noise from the streets below. I recognize the chant which had awakened me each morning in Agra and again in Sawai Madhopur. At first this music had sounded exotic and strange, but by now, there is a familiar, almost comfortable ring to it, and I wonder whether I am on the verge of assimilating into the culture of India.

The reason we are in such a good mood is because we are taking a week off from bicycle travel. Instead we will travel by train to the Seventh Provisional World Parliament in Chennai, a meeting that will reportedly take place in a very nice hotel. So sublime is the thought of a whole week of indulging ourselves in the luxury of not being mobbed, a whole week of complete confidence in the ready availability of regular balanced meals, shelter, maybe even a modicum of cleanliness! My friend, Rani, had only been slightly wrong when she said bicycle travel in India would be impossible. It isn't impossible. It's just difficult.

* * * *

The hotel staff titters among themselves as, with great fanfare, we haul the bike up to our room. Each time we come to a switch back in the narrow stairwell, we have to stand it upright lengthwise on its rear wheel to get it around the corner. As we pass the desk clerk on the second floor, he asks why we don't just keep the bike locked in the entryway. So Dick explains that we are planning to take the whole thing apart and put it in our suitcase. "In suitcase!" He wobbles his head in disbelief. The smile lines in his face explode into laughter. More ripples of laughter follow us as, puffing and grunting, we wrestle our giant blue rabbit all the way up four flights of stairs.

When we get the bike up to the room, Dick takes his tools from the pack and sets to work loosening screws and pulling apart the tubing. I get the bucket from the bathroom and set up shop out on the balcony scrubbing the dust and grime of India off the parts as Dick removes them from the bike. I am in the throes of a scrubbing when Dick comes out and says, "I don't know if I'm going to be able to get all these parts into that suitcase."

Even though he has disassembled and repacked the bike several times before on other trips, I don't question Dick's skepticism. To me it has always seemed like magic, taking this enormous vehicle apart and cramming it into one suitcase. "Maybe I can find another bag in the market," I suggest.

Dick nods. "Yes, we really should have another bag. Anything will do, even an old burlap sack, but it would have to be big enough to hold a bicycle tire,"

"How big?"

"With trained mathematical eyes, Dick surveys one of the tires. "Oh, I'd say about forty by eighty centimeters."

I wonder why a tire is longer than wide, but I never argue with Dick about math. I rip a blank sheet of paper out of my diary and jot down the figures, "40cm x 80cm." Next to that, I make a small sketch of a duffel bag. Then I fold the piece of paper, stuff it into my pocket and head for the streets below.

It is blissful to just walk down the Ujjain Market Street and not be mobbed. Aside from the routine vendors hassling me to buy stuff I don't want and couldn't carry across India on a bicycle even if I did, no one takes much notice of me. I scarcely notice the motorcycles and rickshaws beeping and trying to run me down. It's all so commonplace now. I can concentrate fully upon my search for a bag big enough to hold a bicycle tire. Mostly I eye the stalls in hopes of finding a burlap sack lying around unwanted. That would be cheaper than a new duffel bag. But then I spot something I have not yet seen before in India, a stall hung with a variety of bags and suitcases. It is an Asian style luggage store.

Behind the counter is a small, dark, bearded face with huge spectacles magnifying big sad eyes. Wearing a white Moslem cap and a long, black satin robe, he looks more like a religious celebrant than a street vendor. I approach softly, formidable as I must be to him, this old white lady wearing pants. The eyes gaze across at me dispassionate as a seasoned mariner who senses a storm brewing but is fully equipped to ride it out.

I reach in my pocket, pull out my sketch of the duffel bag and place it on the counter in front of him. "I need a duffel bag," I explain and point to the drawing. "It has to be big enough to hold a bicycle tire." I circumscribe the tire with my hands.

The luggage merchant rolls his patient eyes heavenward. Then he makes an about face and shuffles to the back of his stall, the satin robe swishing back and forth among the merchandise. Soon he returns with a small, shiny, black leather briefcase, large enough to hold a few sheets of legal sized paper but not nearly big enough for a bike tire.

I shake my head and point at my drawing. I am a fairly good draftsman. He should be able to see that I'm looking for an entirely different species of animal. "Duffel bag," I say.

The luggage merchant makes another about face and goes to the back of his stall again. Soon he returns with a perfect specimen of the duffel bag breed. However, it is a pup. I need its pappa. "Yes," I nod. "Duffel bag, but this is too small. It has to hold a bike tire." I pantomime a *bigger circle*. The man brings out several more bags, none large enough for the tire. I keep gesturing bigger. Finally the man climbs up on a stool and pulls out a flat package, even smaller than the original brief case. I keep shaking my head even as he brings the package back and sits it on the counter. Wearing the same sad immutable countenance, he loosens a zipper around three sides of the package, and expands it to the shape of a duffel bag smaller than the first one he had shown me. I shake my head and raise my hand above the duffel bag as if instructing it to grow.

Without saying a word or moving a facial muscle, the bag merchant loosens another zipper and, to my amazement, the bag does grow. He lifts out another section, doubling its size. "It's big enough now," I assure him.

But he is not finished. He unzips another section and then another. Now the bag is so tall, he can barely reach the top, so he sets it on the floor and, without ever altering his expression, continues to expand the bag until it is peering over the counter at me.

"That's certainly big enough," I assure him. "What cost?"

"Three fifty."

"Two fifty?" After all, an old, used burlap sack would do just as well for our purposes as this magical expanding duffel bag.

"Three hundred fifty rupees," he says revealing not the slightest trace of emotion in his voice.

"Three hundred?"

"Three fifty."

So the deal is closed.

Trudging back up the street toward our hotel, I enjoy a fleeting moment of satisfaction about my purchase. I think how clever it was of me to find such a versatile bag. Here it is tucked under my arm, a small inconspicuous object that within seconds could grow large enough to contain an entire disassembled tandem bicycle.

But now I begin to worry. Maybe Dick won't be happy that I spent three hundred and fifty rupees on a fancy expandable bag when a burlap sack would have sufficed. Besides, after carrying the thing awhile, it feels heavier and heavier. Mr. Dick Go-lite might not approve.

When I get back to the hotel room Dick is already packed. He has tied the bicycle tires onto the outside of his backpack. The rest of the bike parts are all fitted like the pieces of a puzzle inside the suitcase.

"I bought a cool bag," I crow proudly. "It's expandable. It could hold the entire bike and much more."

Dick shakes his head. "Too bad. We don't need it after all."

"Oh, no! I paid three fifty for this dumb thing!" I can see the carefully veiled exasperation in those big sad eyes of the vendor when I try to pantomime, "refund." I remember how stubborn he had been about the price.

"Maybe they'll refund the money," Dick suggests.

I shake my head. "You better come with me. I'll need legal counsel to make my case."

I lead Dick back to the luggage stall and let him do the charades. He tries very hard, waving his hands about and tossing out carefully rehearsed Hindi phrases, but he can't even get the vendor to admit he understands that we want our money back. Instead he offers Dick several other suitcases of various sizes and beautiful styles in exchange for the remarkable, expandable duffel bag.

Dick keeps shaking his head. "No, we don't need a bag. We want our money back."

Next the bag wallah begins stabbing his fingers into various corners of the expandable bag to pantomime that he wants us to show him the defect in the merchandise.

"Good bag. Nothing wrong," Dick assures him. "But we don't need a bag. We want our money back." He gestures with that insistent beggar's clawing upward motion like a sea anemone grabbing for food.

The man shakes his head emphatically. "No refund," he says.

I recall how often in India I have encountered street vendors who wouldn't give up on trying to make a sale. I have imagined walking through the market wearing a T-shirt that says, "What part of *no* don't you understand?" All the words would be in Hindi except for the *no* which would be in English. Now the counter is turned the other way. The vendor is saying *no,* but we aren't taking *no* for an answer.

Eventually the bag wallah goes back behind the stall and brings out another man, apparently the boss. We try again, pleading pathetically for our refund. "No refund," he says.

Leaving the bag on the counter, I shrug in resignation and step back away from it. But Dick shoves the piece of merchandise in question toward the boss.

The boss shoves it back again.

Dick shakes his head in a gesture of profound obstinance. "We cannot take this. We are traveling by bicycle. It is too heavy for us to carry."

I am about to call the guy's bluff and turn to walk away without the bag, when suddenly his face contorts into an expression of anguished defeat. He pauses in momentary silence like a preacher meditating in church. Then he opens a drawer beneath the counter and counts out three hundred rupees, laying them in front of us. "Oh, thank you so much," we chortle in unison. Then we bow several times with palms clasped together. "Thank you. Thank you. Namaste." The least we can do is let them keep the other fifty rupees for their trouble.

* * * *

In its own small way, the Ujjain railway station has the same hectic atmosphere as Victoria in Bombay. The floors are covered with dirt and debris to say nothing of one person per square foot charging about in all directions. It's hard to know where to go, whom to ask, what to do. We had been told all trains were booked, but special emergency quotas might be obtained from someone called the railway Superintendent.

Each time we spot someone in a uniform or standing behind a desk, we walk up to them and say, "Superintendent? Where?" The response is always a shrug or head wobble. Finally we spot an official looking window marked, "Reservations and Inquiries." We stand in front of it and wait our turn to obtain directions to the Superintendent's office.

When we finally find the Superintendent's office, a security guard admits us without hesitation.

In contrast with the rest of the station, the Superintendent's office is a paragon of godliness/cleanliness. One wall is hung with a large tapestry of some scene from Hindu mythology. Although the other walls are lined with vacant benches of varnished wood and maroon leather upholstery, all supplicants are huddled in a circle of folding chairs around the Superintendent's desk. The guard motions for us to sit in two of the empty folding chairs.

The gentleman behind the big wooden desk is the essence of importance. He is tall and dignified with a luxurious head of nicely cropped white hair and an impeccable brown suit and tie. Beside him stands a woman in a beautiful orange salwar chemise tunic and pants with gold trim and earrings to match. This seems to be some sort of assistant or secretary.

While we wait our turn to speak with the Superintendent, the security guard brings in an elderly Indian man but does not offer him a seat. The man has a white scruffy beard and tattered clothing, even dirtier than ours had been after biking toward Ujjain yesterday by *the road from hell*. Clearly this gentleman did not have the privilege, as I had last night, of laundering his clothes with Shiny Black Shampoo in a bucket of warm water. The security guard speaks to the attendant who then asks a question of the Superintnedent. The security guard then speaks to the elderly gentleman and back and forth awhile until finally the disappointed old man is ushered back out of the room. I'm glad I have perfected the laundry technique so well and have made us look so spiffy clean. Otherwise we may not have been admitted either. On the other hand, I suspect the fairness of our skin may have even more to do with our privilege than the cleanliness of our attire.

When our turn comes to speak with the Superintendent, Dick explains that we need emergency quota reservations because we have been traveling in India and are due to attend a meeting in Chennai on the 26th of December. The Superintendent says, "You must first go to the Reservations and Inquiries office and make a reservation. Then come back here and apply for an emergency quota."

Dick says, "We have just come from the Reservations office. They told us to come here."

The Superintendent shakes his head and repeats, "You must first go to the Reservations office and make a reservation. Then you can come here to apply for the quota."

After we wait in line at Reservations and Inquiries, the clerk gives us a form to fill out and motions us into another line. When our turn finally comes in that line, I can hear the clerk explaining various options to Dick. If I were closer and wearing my hearing aids, I might have a prayer of understanding what he says despite his thick, rapid Hindi accent and the surrounding background noise. Fortunately, Dick does seem to understand and fills out the form. We return to the Superintendent's office and wait in the chairs some more.

When our turn comes again, the Superintendent looks at Dick's form, nods and says, "Now you need to apply for the quota."

"How do we apply? Is there a form?" Dick asks.

The Superintendent seems baffled by the question. He shakes his head in a manner suggesting that everyone in India must be born knowing how to write a proper letter of application. "No form. You must write your application on paper."

We fumble about in our packs, but we have no paper. I tear a blank page out of my diary. While the Superintendent attends to another customer, Dick crafts a note explaining that we need to apply for an emergency quota, signs it at the bottom, and hands it back to the Superintendent.

The Superintendent looks at the note and shakes his head. Then he turns the paper over, points at the bottom of the page and says, "Please sign."

Although we are totally mystified, Dick signs his name at the bottom of the blank side of the paper and hands it back.

The Superintendent shakes his head again. Then he points to the top of the page and says, "Please print your name and address." Senseless as it all seems, Dick obeys, and the Superintendent is finally satisfied. "Good," he says. "You must come back at four o'clock this afternoon to find out whether your quota is approved."

"Did you understand what that was all about?" I ask Dick as we leave the station.

"Not really," he says. "Maybe they wanted it on official letterhead."

"I hope it gets approved."

"I hope so too. The train leaves at five."

CHAPTER 13

Christmas Day in Chennai

Yes, we were granted the emergency quota, and so we emerge from Chennai Central train station as planned, very early Christmas morning. We are a different pair, however, than the bumbling novices that had stumbled out of the Bombay airport nearly a month ago. I don't know whether we have yet achieved Gandhian humility, but we know how to avoid harassment. It's a matter of staring straight ahead at some imagined vision of the center of the universe.

Placidly we shuffle along, Dick pulling our big suitcase through deep layers of plastic bags and garbage. With yogic concentration, we glance neither to the left nor right and sashay around a man who sits on the sidewalk warming his hands over a fire of burning plastic, inhaling the toxic fumes as though they were pure oxygen. We scarcely hear the chorus of voices hassling us for the privilege of carrying our luggage. Oblivious to the tug of hands grabbing for my duffel bag, I just walk right by as if we were alone in the mountains of Washington State.

The guidebook says that historic Fort St. George, built in 1653 by the East India Company, is quite close by, so we head for it via the sidewalk in front of the medical school womens' dormitory. Even though the sidewalk is fairly wide, Dick has to walk in the street with the suitcase to avoid foot high sewer covers and big gaps in the sidewalk from which the smell of raw sewage escapes into the warm, dry air.

We cross the busy street on a pedestrian overpass and follow a walkway that mercifully removes us from the chaotic din of traffic. On one side of the path a spindly grove of trees grows out of dry, littered soil.

We enter the Fort through an archway where a placard on a stone wall blackened with soot and smelling of urine, informs us that this historic place is being preserved for posterity. My soul momentarily leaves this scene as memory takes me back to a gray Christmas morning in the meadow surrounding our cabin on Hood Canal in Washington State. Acres of shimmering wet grass and giant cedar trees spread before me, dark and pure without a trace of litter. In the far flung future that scene may change. There may come a day when that land also succumbs to the pressure this one has felt of over-population, poverty, and neglect.

Coming out of Fort St. George on the front side, we line up to hail an auto-rickshaw in front of a Napoleonic mansion built by the city's founder, Robert Clive. Towering above us is a flag pole that was once the mast of a wrecked ship, complete with platforms, walkways, and rope ladders for climbing about in the sky above the ocean. It now serves as a flag pole, flying the orange and green colors of India over a raging torrent of city traffic.

We hail an auto-rickshaw, cram our luggage and ourselves into the back seat, and show the driver our printout of the Palm Grove Hotel's web page. He nods and we flit off like a piece of flotsam into the flood. There aren't many more handholds on a rickshaw than there had been on Sant Doss' motorcycle. It is basically a double seat on a three-wheeled motorcycle. I hang onto Dick's arm and try to think of this as a carnival ride. I am a child, having spent my allowance to experience the thrill of speed and danger. A motorcycle races by carrying a real little girl about four years old. Wearing a pink ruffled dress, she sits on the handle bars in front of her father. Helmets and seat belts have yet to be invented.

* * * *

Eating our Christmas morning breakfast at the Palm Grove Hotel Restaurant, I think I must have died and gone to a heaven of cleanliness/godliness. The walls are decorated with marble and mirrors that reflect the light of decorative fixtures whose wiring is hidden from view. There is not a speck of humble dust in sight. I finish off a couple of pasty, unsweetened pancakes, rather missing our usual menu of boiled eggs and bananas, seasoned with a bit of road dust.

We sip our tea and visit with two new friends, Mr. Shradesh and Mr. Menom, who are also here to attend the Seventh Provisional World Parliament. Mr. Shradesh's sturdy, well-padded frame is adorned with a gray, western style suit and tie. Mr. Menom is a slender gentleman with white hair and soft intelligent eyes. He wears a simple Indian style shirt with a Nehru collar. Mr. Menom gifts me with a signed copy of his novel entitled *Rohila's Resolution* and recommends another book he has written about his peace walk around the world.

Mr. Shradesh shows us his photo album. Every frame contains a consciously posed image of himself standing with one or more important personages. He points to every frame, identifying each person by name, title and rank. Most are presidents of the Rotary and Lions Clubs in his hometown. Several are businessmen. Another is a representative to the Tamil Nadu parliamentary assembly. Finally he turns to a photo of himself standing beside an equally prosperous and healthy looking woman about his age.

"Is this your wife?" asks Dick.

"Oh, no. I am not married. I give my life to spiritual practice and service to the community. This is Madame Kapur. She is a powerful woman, very well-known in my city."

"Powerful? Is she the mayor?" I ask.

Mr. Shradesh laughs. "Oh, no. Mrs. Kapur is my guru. She has great spiritual power. She goes for weeks without eating, sleeping, or drinking but is nevertheless quite healthy."

I shake my head in amazement. From the photo, Mrs. Kapur's beautiful red silk sari appears quite full of her abundant female form.

"That is amazing!" I say.

"Yes, truly amazing," Mr. Shradesh agrees. "Mrs. Kapur is also clairvoyant. Upon first meeting you, she can tell you all about your life and your children."

"How do you suppose she does this?" asks Dick in a characteristic tone of skepticism.

Mr. Shradesh smiles and closes his eyes as if to demonstrate. "She spends weeks and months in meditation without ever eating or sleeping. I try to imitate her, but it is difficult. I am totally abstinent of alcohol and sex. I meditate several hours each day. But I must work to supplement my income."

"What kind of work do you do?" I ask.

"I am a retired biologist. But I am also a distributor of soap," he says. "A miracle product called Amway."

"Ah, yes. I have heard of Amway. We have it in America." I have used it once or twice in my washing machine at home. It is highly concentrated and very expensive. I look again at Mr. Shradesh's pressed suit and spotlessly clean shirt. "Do you do your own laundry with Amway?" I ask.

"Oh, yes."

"How do you do it?"

"How?"

"Do you use a bucket of water in the bathroom?"

Mr. Shradesh looks at me as though he considers my question a little strange. Then he shrugs. "Yes, of course. How else would I do it?" Perhaps I should try to buy a small amount of Amway from Mr. Shradesh to take with us on the bike, but on the other hand, Shiny Black shampoo seems to work.

Mr. Shradesh continues to introduce us to the other famous personages in his photo album, but my attention is drawn to a young man busing the tables. He takes dishes away in a round plastic tub about three feet in diameter. I have noticed a number of these tubs around this hotel. Waiters use them to carry food to the rooms or to the roof garden. But I have begun to imagine an even better use for one of these receptacles.

"Will you please excuse me," I say to Mr. Shradesh. "I have to talk with the manager."

Mr. Shradesh nods at me and smiles. The three men continue to chat about Mr. Shradesh's guru, but they are all watching me. Everyone in the restaurant is watching me stand in the middle of the restaurant talking to the gentleman who seems to be in charge.

I try to speak softly, so not all of them can hear. "May I speak with the manager?" I ask.

The man's head bobs back and forth several times. "I am manager," he says.

"Good. I would like to ask a great favor."

"Yes?"

"I would like to borrow one of these tubs." I point across the room to the tub that is still being carried about to bus the tables.

"You want to borrow what?"

"A tub." I point to it again.

"You want a tub for what?"

"For a bath."

"You have a tub in your room, Madame." He is referring to the bucket in our bathroom. It is large enough to contain my feet but nothing else. There is a small hot water heater in the room with a switch to turn it on. We have been promised that in less than half an hour it will heat enough water to fill the bucket several times. If I only had this tub, I could soak my bottom in it, maybe even my elbows and part of my back while my feet are simultaneously immersed in the bucket of hot water. It would not exactly replicate my bath tub at home, but it would feel like heaven.

How can I make the man understand? I have never been a shower person. I have always been totally incapable of understanding why a shower, water spraying from above, can be compared in any way to a bath. A shower may clean the skin, but a bath soothes every aching muscle and releases the pent-up stress in every neuron. At home I do a yogic meditation in the bath tub that cinches the ethereal experience of disembodiment.

Obviously I cannot speak Hindi, or for that matter any language well enough to explain the amenities of bathing. So I look pleadingly into the man's eyes, hoping he will grasp how important this is to me. Then I say, pointing to the tub, "I will sit in that. I will put my feet in the smaller tub. It will feel like my bathtub at home in America. I have been away from home bicycling across India for a month. I am homesick for my bathtub."

The man's expression softens. He nods sympathetically, almost as if he does understand or maybe believes that I have some strange affliction. "Yes, Madame." He points to the tub. "We will bring it to your room this afternoon."

"Oh thank you, so much!" I exclaim and return to the table.

Mr. Shradesh has closed his photo album and is taking his leave. "So pleased to meet you Doctor Dick," he says. "You must bicycle to Nellore some day and meet Mrs. Kapur."

"I would like to meet her," Dick says, "But Nellore isn't on our route."

I call to Mr. Shradesh's back as he departs, "So happy to meet you. See you later, Mr. Shradesh." Maybe I have missed an opportunity for a real Indian guru adventure while conspiring to recreate my surrogate spiritual practice of taking a bath.

After Mr. Shradesh is out of hearing range, Dick says, "I wonder whether this Mrs. Kapur is for real."

Mr. Menom shrugs. "Perhaps," he says. "There are a lot of religious wonders in India. Many are scientifically proven to be authentic. Some are fakes."

"How do people tell the difference?" I ask.

Mr. Menom laughs. "It doesn't matter. If you want to become a guru in India, all you have to do is go sit on a street corner and say you are a person of god. People will feed you."

Dick nods knowingly and breaths a sigh of satisfaction. He has finally met a fellow skeptic in India.

"I wonder whether there will be any gurus attending the Seventh Provisional World Parliament," I say.

"There will be a good many at the opening ceremony. Lots of people will want to have their pictures taken with the Chief Justice who will officiate. By noon tomorrow most of them will be gone, even Mr. Shradesh."

It crosses my mind that Mr. Menom is even more skeptical than Dick. "I hope some of the gurus stay. I want to meet one," I say.

"You will meet Yogi Shanti Swaroop. He's quite a character. You will like him."

"Is he legitimate or a fraud?" I ask.

"Swami Shanti Swaroop is quite himself. He believes he is what he says he is. So, if he's a fraud, it's not intentional," laughs Mr. Menom.

"If he isn't what he believes he is, he must be crazy," observes Dick.

Mr. Menom shrugs. "Sometimes I think there is a fine line between religion and craziness. For instance today, in the Christian world, lots of people are literally celebrating a virgin birth."

"They can't all be crazy," I insist.

* * * *

Coming out of the restaurant, Dick and I stop at the hotel registration desk to ask whether we have received any mail. We wait in eager anticipation while the clerk searches the mail slots, finally materializing one small package. Reading over Dick's shoulder, I note that the package is from Boston. The good news is I have my care package from my daughter. The bad news is we still have no inner tubes.

Dick groans in bitter disappointment. "I'll have to email them again."

I share Dick's frustration about the inner tubes, but I'm so excited to receive Dana's Christmas present that I sit down immediately on a couch in the hotel lobby and rip it open. There are three large packs of baby wipes, three giant bags of wild cherry cough drops, and to my incalculable joy, three spools of strong, white, unwaxed dental floss. Santa has arrived on the morning of December 25! This is the most valuable Christmas gift I have ever received.

* * * *

The Lakme Beauty Salon is, in many ways, a western style experience. Unlike beauty shops I have passed in smaller towns, this one has four complete walls. There is even a separate waiting room with a desk. My guess is that Lakme might be part of a chain operation because they have storage shelves, walls and literature imprinted with their logo. The prices are almost western style with a cut and perm topping out at the equivalent of twenty five dollars. That's more than a poor Indian family comes by in a couple of weeks.

The wait for my perm is long enough to read much of Mr. Menom's novel which is quite a thriller, calling to mind a once popular T-Shirt message, "Ladies Sewing Circle and Terrorist Society." The heroine is a sweet, young woman who gets mixed up with a bunch of radical leftists. She plans to knock off the Indian Minister of Finance for selling out to U.S. capitalist imperialism. This seems to be an odd plot for someone like Mr. Menom who has a gentle demeanor and who, skeptic or not, purports to be a follower of Gandhi.

By the time I make it out of the waiting room and into the salon area, I am ready for a less compelling read, so I pick up a copy of the Indian version of *New Woman* magazine which, surprisingly, also holds my interest. The cover story features a woman in western exercise attire holding a basketball. The title proclaims, "Be Your Own Life Coach." The target audience is an emerging population of modern career women, the like of which I have not encountered since the newspaper reporter in Agra. The author advises them not to try to be superwomen but to make time for themselves, elicit housekeeping help from other members of the family, presumably their husbands, and try not to let their careers ruin their lives. The other major article is about how to keep a journal to help work out personal issues, express yourself creatively, or just keep a record of your life. Even though, as an old American granny type, I am not the target audience, I feel the article speaks to me. After all, I am keeping a journal myself.

So my wait here has been pleasant and not a waste of time. Besides reading about affluent young Indian women, I have the opportunity to observe some in real life. Most of the customers are young women of movie-star caliber glamour. They are dressed in western style clothing. Some have taken off outer garments to allow their long dark legs to protrude languidly from beneath smart little mini-skirts. Their perfect bodies are crowned with voluptuous manes of *Shiny Black* hair much like the one on the shampoo bottle. They lounge comfortably about in an attitude that says they are accustomed to being waited on. One of them is having her feet soaked in a plastic bowl, presumably to prepare for a pedicure. Another's luxurious locks are being separately brushed with a thick greasy substance as they lay on long strands of red plastic. Although back home I spend two hours per quarter in a beauty shop for my regular cut and perm, I have never before observed such a variety of mysterious cosmetological operations. Cuts, sets, perms and now and then a color job is the extent of my beautician's repertoire.

At long last, my turn has come and the beautician leads me to her chair in the center of the room. Although there are three or four worker bees, this seems to be the only real beautician. The others appear to be her assistants or perhaps apprentices. They busy themselves making sure all the rollers have fasteners, handing her the curling papers, sweeping hair off customers.

The real beautician is a short, stout woman appearing more Vietnamese or some such variety of Asian, rather than Indian. That concerns me because I have not had good luck with Asian hair dressers in my predominantly Vietnamese neighborhood in Seattle. No matter how hard I have tried to communicate with them, I always come out with a mop of tight frizz instead of the body wave I asked for. They don't seem to grasp that my reason for wanting a perm is not to get tight curls. The purpose is to transform my fine filmy veil into the illusion of a thick smart "do"—like theirs.

The beautician drapes a big plastic apron over me and lays out an array of skinny little rollers.

I examine them with misgivings. "Do you have larger ones?" I gesture bigger.

She shakes her head. "Big rollers no make good curls."

"I don't want curls. I want a body wave, very little curl." For the past thirty years I have worn a pixie style requiring no more maintenance than an occasional shampoo. That requires a short cut with a very loose body wave done with the largest rollers on the market.

She laughs and picks up a curler as skinny as Scrooge's little pinky. "Biggest size," she insists.

"Okay, but don't leave the lotion on too long."

Not leaving the lotion on proves not to be an option. She has too many customers.

To divert my attention from the chemical destruction of my hair, I return to Menom's thriller novel. By the time the beautician returns with her bottle of neutralizer, Rohila has thrown a hand grenade at the Finance Minister in the middle of a press conference.

Tugging and pulling at my hair, the beautician removes all the rollers. An old white version of Li'l Orphan Annie with my mother's granny face frowns at me from the mirror.

I know what I have to do. The solution to this problem is even simpler than Rohila's. It's crew cut time. I will have her assassinate everyone of those tiny tendrils.

The beautician picks up the scissors. "How you want cut?"

"Pixie style, very, very short."

"Very short?"

"Very!"

She shakes her head. "Make beautiful curls. Then cut off?" It's a familiar argument.

But she begins to cut and cut.

After awhile she asks, "Enough?"

"More."

She cuts more—and more.

Like seeds from a cotton wood tree, the white hair flies about us tickling my nostrils and covering the plastic apron.

After she has cut enough to suit me, the beautician fluffs her stubby fingers through the white lamb fuzz barely covering my scalp and sighs with satisfaction, "Very nice!" Then she looks at one of her young glamorous charges lounging nearby and declares, "Next time I make for you!"

CHAPTER 14

Seventh Provisional World Parliament

Eugenia, the Secretary, towers over the podium dismantling the microphone several times in an effort to adjust it to her gangly height. The entire wall behind her is covered with a big banner that reads, "Seventh Provisional World Parliament." Clothed in a long black skirt and white cotton blouse with four columns of ruffles, Eugenia is an agreeably androgynous American who connects with my imagination in some inexplicably spiritual way like the reincarnation of a sweet Tennessee Walker horse that was my daughter's dearest childhood friend. It must be those big kind eyes peering over plain rimmed spectacles, the long blond mane of hair refusing to be contained by the white bandana tied pirate-like around her head, the sinewy athletic arms, the long boney neck and face framed in dangling gold earrings.

Narrow expressive lips open wide to expose a large set of teeth as she explains at length several recommended changes to the International Criminal Court laws to prosecute perpetrators of war crimes. "The Rome statute was well drafted," she says, "But without benefit of knowledge of the Constitution for the Federation of the Earth." Everyone nods in solemn agreement. We follow along on printed sheets as Eugenia reads her new wording that would incorporate the Constitution.

These people have long since adopted their own Constitution as legitimate world law despite the fact that only a small segment of the world's population has ever heard of it. "Section forty-five," she says, "Requires solemn undertaking by judges, attorneys, and registrars to affirm and uphold the Earth Constitution."

This week of meetings is an exercise in what seems like futility. These are all intelligent, supposedly sane people, the couple dozen or so scattered about a nearly empty meeting hall on this warm afternoon. They must all know there is really no democratic world government based upon the beautifully crafted Constitution for the Federation of the Earth. But they have suspended belief for a cause they love. Some of them have spent as many as five decades promoting this ideal.

Dick and I listen and nod approvingly at appropriate times just as we have bowed reverently before the images of deities in so many temples along the way. This seems to be a sort of ritual, much like the offering of lamps and ringing of bells before the shrines of Shiva, Ganesh, and scores of other gods. But on the other hand, we know that one day there will be a democratically elected global parliament. Any practice aimed at keeping that dream alive is surly worth the effort, no matter how silly it may seem to some. Maybe "Bike for Global Democracy" seems even sillier to a lot of people. A couple of old Don Quixotes we are, tilting at windmills.

We are well into the afternoon of the second to last day. The windowless room is adequately lit by subtle overhead lighting. The temperature is warm enough to make me feel sleepy, but not uncomfortably so, even though the only source of air seems to be a doorway at the back which opens onto the roof garden.

In front of the room beside Eugenia at the podium is a table where the other officers, each gentlemen with his own table microphone, sit in suits and sport jackets facing the meeting hall. Planted in the first Chair is Dr. Amerisinghe, an elderly gentleman from Sri Lanka, looking solid and earthy as a big stump of Washington State Douglas Fir, complete with fungal nodes and dark, shaggy bark. But ringing out from his solid form is a voice that could compete in pitch and volume with a marmot whistle. Next to him is Dr. Glenn Martin, a philosophy professor from Virginia, a well-spoken baby boomer, every inch of him, including the curly gray beard, looking disciplined and well cared for with proper diet and regular exercise.

I have started to drift off when Eugenia arouses me by dismantling and reassembling the microphone again creating a buzzing in the system even more alarming than Mr. Amerisinghe's voice. "Part Five, Investigation and Prosecution. Section fifty-nine defines arrest proceedings in the custodial State during Provisional World Government and first operative stage of World Government."

I am further awakened by a stirring across the aisle. Attendance is sparse in contrast with the packed meeting room we had encountered on the first morning of the inaugural ceremonies. One row of seats is dominated by a contingent of teenaged boys from the City Montessori School of Lucknow. All dressed for success in blue suits, white shirts and ties, they vary in developmental stature from the dawn of puberty to broad-chested maturity. The smallest and most outspoken one appears in size and stature to be little more than twelve but has wisdom, grace and intelligence far beyond his years. He raises his hand. "Dr. Amerasinghe, I request that the Chair to allow me to speak on the issue of penalties," he says.

The boys are great speech makers and, by far, the most active participants. Maybe that's because of their proximity to the time in life for playing games of dramatic pretense. In fact, if the Seventh Provisional World Parliament achieves nothing else, it provides a great arena for these boys to play at being parliamentarians. They appear to be the only ones who have reviewed all the legislative recommendations beforehand and have come with prepared remarks.

"Are you certain this is relevant to the topic?" Mr. Amerisinghe's shrill soprano rings out like an alarm bell bringing everyone to attention. While the boys' speeches have always been delivered with the aplomb and polish of professional politicians, they have sometimes been off the subject. Earlier, the big one had launched into a diatribe against child labor until Professor Martin assured him that such practices were already overruled by the Constitution for the Federation of the Earth.

"My comment does not relate to penalties, exactly," said the boy. "In fact, there is nothing in the statute that covers my concern."

"We must stay on the subject or we will not finish with the Rome Statute today," whines Mr. Amerisinghe. He looks around at the rest of us as if hoping for support. Mr. Menom is there and, despite Menom's skeptical prediction, so is Mr. Shradesh. Near the end of our row is a rotund Indian woman about my age who was introduced to me as a medical doctor although I don't recall her name. Next to her sits Professor Chavan, a white-headed gentleman wearing a gold Nehru suit. Neither of them have spoken very often, but when they do, it is in hushed tones of profound wisdom.

"Respectfully, Mr. Chair, please let him speak," says Professor Chavan. "He is a legitimate delegate to this provisional parliament." We all nod agreement.

Mr. Amerisinghe says, "Very well, please make your comment brief."

"My comment relates to rehabilitation. There is nothing in the Statute about how we will rehabilitate these criminals to peaceful, productive citizenship."

Now I am really awake. The corners of my mouth curl into a smirk as I imagine Slobodan Milosevic, Saddam Hussein or even George Bush sentenced by the International Criminal Court to study Gandhian philosophy at the City Montessori School in Lucknow.

Professor Chavan and the medical doctor both nod in solemn agreement. Everyone else follows suit.

Eugenia's eyes light up. "You are certainly right! What a terrible oversight! Why has no one else ever thought of that? I suggest that you work with us on another revision of this Statute to present at the Eighth Provisional World Parliament. That will be held next year in . . ."

Eugenia looks up, distracted by something in the back of the room. She drops the microphone which emits an intense whistle. Her big eyes open wide, and her long, thin lips part in a radiant smile. The boy's head turns along with everyone else's to find out what she is looking at.

All eyes follow the figure parading like a bride groom down the center aisle. He is a short waif of a fellow and almost completely bald with beads and medallions adorning his bare-chest. He wears only a dhoti tucked up between his legs, much like popular photos of Gandhi. The corners of his mouth protrude into round plump cheeks forming a grin that connotes either mindlessness or a state of holy enlightenment. It would be hard for the untrained and unenlightened to tell.

As he approaches the podium, Eugenia apologizes, "I'm so sorry, but I must pause to introduce someone who has just arrived. We expected him this morning but his plane was delayed. This is Swami Shanti Swaroop. I met Swami Swaroop when he came to America where he has been teaching for many years. But now he has returned to India where he will withdraw from earthly pleasures and give himself entirely to meditation and spiritual practice in his final days on this planet."

Swami Swaroop climbs up onto the platform where he turns and bows at us with palms pressed together. We all bow back and say, "Namaste."

Other than that, everyone, including the Swami, is pretty much speechless.

"I had hoped that you could come this morning to lead us in a short meditation before the session," says Eugenia. She looks at her watch. "I'm sorry your plane was delayed. But since it's time for our afternoon tea, perhaps you would do the honors now."

Without saying a word, Swami Swaroop folds himself into a lotus flower on the platform facing the assembly. All eyes close in an attitude of meditation as the Swami begins to chant in the luxurious tenor, "Oooooooooooom Shantiiiiiiiiiiiii Oooooooooooom" he sings in a voice that would rival an opera star's rendition of the National Anthem in Yankee Stadium. So what if Swami Swaroop says very little? His three syllable chant could put the entire neighborhood into an instant trance.

* * * *

Chai glasses in hand we arrange ourselves into various groupings during the break. Dick chats with Dr. Chavan and several of the boys. The Swami stands between Eugenia and the medical doctor. He sidles up close to Eugenia in a way that seems comically coquettish in view her contrasting height. After a while, he turns to the medical doctor and flashes a flirty grin. It appears that this holy man may not yet have given up all entirely earthly pleasures heralding the end of his days on this planet.

I find myself standing next to Professor Martin. "What do you think of the Constitution for the Federation of the Earth? Have you had time to read it yet?" he asks.

"I received my copy only yesterday. I am still studying it. The Constitution is a remarkable document," I say. "The author, Phillip Eisley, is truly a genius."

"Phillip Eisley is only the editor. The Constitution has been written with input from people all over the world. It is a labor of over half a century of international cooperation."

I nod and smile. Several speakers had mentioned this during the inaugural ceremonies.

"So, are you ready to endorse the Constitution?" he asks.

"Oh yes, I endorse it heartily," I assure him. "But our approach is a little different. Dick and I believe this may actually be the Constitution that will be adapted by the future World Parliament. On the other hand it seems to us more likely that there will be a new document developed at the time using this and others as a model."

"In the mean time will you be promoting the Constitution for the Federation of the Earth as you bicycle around the world?"

"To some extent we will. But to us it seems important not to designate this as the final document. When the time comes to elect a real world parliament, it must be by a democratic process occurring at the time. For example, we think a world parliament could be started with as few as twenty countries signing onto a treaty. Those countries would hold a constitutional convention to draft their operational document . . ."

My sentence is interrupted by a waiter offering me another glass of chai. Meanwhile one of the boys calls Professor Martin aside to ask him a question and he seems glad to be rid of the conversation. Hoping I have not said anything to offend Professor Martin, I take my fresh glass and walk over to Dick who is now talking with Eugenia. The Swami still listens attentively to the doctor.

"You have done a remarkable job of drafting legislation for this conference," Dick says to Eugenia.

"Yes, it's amazing," I agree. "Where did you learn the skill?" Even though I know she is a high school social studies teacher back in New York, I figure Eugenia must have been in law school or served in the legislature in an another life. With very little help from anyone, she had drafted all the resolutions to be passed at this conference

"I learned from the Internet. I can show you the web sites."

"I should have known. Don't we learn everything from the Internet these days? I would like to know these web sites," I say.

"If you both come by my room this evening after dinner, I can show it to you. I can also show you legislation we have passed at the other six sessions of the Provisional Parliament. Maybe you can help draft some bills for the Eighth Provisional World Parliament in Lucknow next year?"

Dick says, "I have to use the Internet this evening to catch up on my email, but I think I'd better go down the street to the Internet café for that. Maybe Mona could visit with you while I go out to the Internet café."

"Of course. She's welcome."

"Yes, thank you for the invitation." I agree hesitantly. I want to make it clear that a visit is all I'm volunteering for. Eugenia must need help. It must be a big job to write all the laws needed to justly and effectively govern the entire planet. I have a weakness for joining organizations and getting over my head in volunteer work. Besides, another trip to India next year may not be in our budget. We have other Bike for Global Democracy trips planned for Europe and Brazil.

* * * *

It isn't difficult to find Eugenia's room. It is next door to ours. In fact, we few Americans attending the conference seem to be located in the same hallway. Perhaps that's why the man who shines shoes has stationed himself at the junction to this corridor. He pesters me on the average of four times a day, claiming that my shoes are very dirty and need to be shined. He approaches me again as I knock on Eugenia's door. "Shine shoes, Madame!" he insists even though I am wearing white sneakers.

When Eugenia appears at the door, he calls in to her, "Shine shoes, Madame!" We hurriedly escape into the room and close the door.

"Welcome! I'm so glad we can have this time together," she says.

"Yes, thanks for inviting me." I feel a special affinity for Eugenia. We women activists for global democracy are rare.

Eugenia's laptop computer sits on her only chair, so we sit down on her bed opposite the chair and gaze across at the screen. "The Internet connection has been pretty good here," she says, instantly calling up an Oregon site on drafting legislation. Each time she comes to a new site, I jot down the web address on a blank page of my diary. I am not sure I will ever use this information, but it is interesting to discover a new source of knowledge, skill, and power.

I have not tired of the process when Eugenia closes her laptop and places it on a shelf above her bed. Then she offers me the empty chair which I accept as she sits back down on the edge of her bed. She looks intently at the wall beside my head as if she is trying to think of the right words to tell me something. Finally she says, "I'm so glad you and Dick came to Chennai. I know it is way off your bike route and must have thrown your schedule off."

"Oh, no! I'm so glad to be here! I would not have missed this for the world!" I recall that we had come at her suggestion by email to Dick. She had learned from a global democracy list serve that we would be traveling at this time in India.

"That's good," she says. "I'm glad you feel it was worthwhile. But I have been thinking it was wrong for me to invite you and Dick to come as delegates for next year's session in Lucknow."

"Oh? Why?" I am not disappointed. I had no intention of going, but I feel a sense of rejection for being uninvited.

"It's great to have you here, and I hope you will come next year as observers. Your input is most valuable. But, you see, delegates need to be people who are committed to the Constitution for the Federation of the Earth and who believe in its legitimacy as the basis for World Government."

"Oh, I see. Yes, I understand fully," I say, feeling relieved. Euguenia likes us and wants our company, but we don't subscribe to the belief system of these people. But then I wonder. Surely Mr. Menom doesn't either. In fact, probably Professor Chavan doesn't and who knows how many of the others? But unlike me, they are more diplomatic, careful not to shatter anyone else's dream. Perhaps it was my remarks this afternoon to Professor Martin, or per-

haps other hapless remarks Dick and I have made off and on throughout the week. Although we feel a strong affinity with these people
whose ideals are like ours in so many ways, our world view doesn't
fit inside of theirs. "It's alright, I say. We can't come to India next
year anyway. Our travel budget will be spent on a trip to Brazil for
the 2005 World Social Forum. I hope you will be there, Eugenia. I
hope you will join our coalition for a world parliament."

"I'll try. But I cannot promise because . . ." As Eugenia speaks,
there is a knock on the door. She gets up to open it.

Swami Shanti Swaroop stands in the door jamb wearing his most
benevolent grin.

Eugenia's eyes light up as they had when the Swami showed up
at the meeting this afternoon and something tells me it's time for
me to go. Three is a crowd.

                              * * * *

I take my leave to find Dick at the Internet café. Unlike most
Internet cafés in India, you don't have to climb a narrow, makeshift
staircase and duck under rafter beams to get to this one. It's located
in a kind of shopping mall of little stalls with its own bicycle parking lot in front. Luckily, there is an empty seat next to Dick's, so I
start to call up my own email which I have not read for several days.
But as I sit down, I notice that Dick is really excited. He is smiling,
jotting down notes on scratch paper, making calculations. "What's
up?" I say.

"Wow!" he says. "This is better than I expected. We have four-
teen speakers for our global democracy panel at the World Social
Forum in Mumbai. All the other guys doing workshops on global
democracy have agreed to be on our panel. They all like our idea of
starting a Coalition."

"That's wonderful!" I say. I don't feel so rejected now. The Provisional World Parliament group is just one small band of idealists.
With so many groups around the world thinking about global democracy, there must be a coalition out there someplace.

CHAPTER 15

Dark Night of Body and Soul

We leave the Seventh Provisional World Parliament on the night train from Chennai to Hyderabad. There we will transfer to another train for Aurangabad to resume our bike trip to Bombay.

I awaken on the top bunk in a fit of sneezing. Beside me in the darkness are three large wads of handkerchief completely soaked in slimy mucus. My head is swollen. My nose feels like a boil with pus running out. The inside of one nostril is covered with scabs and the other bleeds intermittently.

I have felt this brewing for some time, but it came to a head on our last day out of Chennai during a bus excursion into the countryside. As our tourist bus plowed through dingy little towns stopping at ancient carvings and temple sights like Mamallapuram and the cottage silk industry of Kanchipuram, my nose got worse. I stopped to buy the three handkerchiefs that hung from the rafters of a vendor stall, but they were soaked in no time. So I had to continue swiping stacks of table napkins from restaurants.

I have had a few sinus infections in my adult life although none have been this severe. They have always hit when I was traveling outside the moist, relatively clean air of the Pacific Northwest. Everyone says I should see a doctor and get some antibiotics, but I don't believe in antibiotics. The best cure for infection is to stay healthy, eat well, get lots of exercise, and the body will heal itself. Fighting off an infection will thereby develop more natural antibodies to fight off future infections. I call this the "immunology theory." I don't know how scientifically sound it is, but so far it has worked for me. I have not taken antibiotics for at least twenty years.

Meanwhile I dope up on antihistamine trying to reduce the symptoms to a tolerable level and just keep going. Unfortunately, at the moment I'm double-dosed on the strongest antihistamines I could get from a drug store wallah in Chennai, but I am still miserable. All three handkerchiefs are completely soaked, so I blow my nose into a spare, clean T-shirt. The antihistamine overdose will put me to sleep soon. Breathing slowly in and out through my mouth, I close my eyes in the darkness and try to think of nothing but the gentle rocking of the train and the hum of its wheels on the track.

* * * *

I am suddenly awakened by Dick's big, strong hand, tugging at my elbow. "Mona, wake up," he gasps. I can hear him panting and moaning very close to my face.

This is very strange for Dick. Panting and moaning have never been part of his behavioral repertoire.

"What's wrong? You sound bad," I say.

"Yes. I'm very sick," he whispers and crumples back onto the lower bunk.

I roll over and climb down to him. "How sick? What's wrong?" I whisper for fear of waking other passengers.

"My abdomen hurts bad," he groans.

"We'll have to get off the train and take you to the doctor."

"It'll be morning in a couple of hours. We'll get off in Hyderabad," he says. "Didn't you bring along some pain pills?"

That's when I recall the pain pills Joan had given me. "Take these along," she had said. "They'll get you through anything. In India, it may be a long way to a doctor." All these weeks I have carried those pills around in a small canvas bag of toiletries inside the daypack that is so inseparable from myself as to be part of my identity. I have no idea whether or not the pills will work, but I find them easily, even now in the darkness. So many weeks of traveling have honed my "blind skills" to perfection. I deftly place the pills in Dick's mouth and hand him the white plastic water bottle.

"Thanks," he says. He moans again while tilting the bottle toward his mouth.

"Is there anything else I can do?" I ask.

"I guess not," he says, "Not now. There'll be a doctor in Hyderabad."

"Sure. I hope the pills help," I say. Then I climb back up to my bunk.

By this time the pressure has built up in my nose again, so I have to blow into my T-shirt again. Even in the darkness, I can see blood stains, looking black on the white cotton shirt. Will I ever get it clean in a bucket of cold water using *Shiny Black* shampoo?

The weird thing about all this is that the many warnings we had received about health problems in India had all been framed in the context of diarrhea. I fully expected to have diarrhea most of the time. I was diagnosed with chronic colitis several years ago. Loose bowels are therefore a normal part of my daily life back home. But in India I have not yet had any serious diarrhea. In fact, because of the starchy, low-bulk diet, I have often experienced the opposite symptom. I have been bothered by lack of appetite, coughing, and severe nasal congestion, but not the runs.

Another pressing concern is what will happen when we get to Aurangabad. Professor Chavan had mentioned something to Dick about our visiting his experimental farm outside Aurangabad, staying there with him, visiting the ancient cave temples at Ajanta and Ellora, maybe even speaking at the college. These illnesses weaken our chances of such a dream scenario really taking place. We'll arrive in Aurangabad much later than expected, if at all. Even then, we may be in no condition to speak before a large educated audience.

* * * *

When everyone else has left the train in the Hyderabad Station, Dick is still lying on his bunk, barely able to move. Already draped with my part of the luggage, namely my back pack, duffel bag, and two panniers, I stand beside him wondering what to do. A small but sturdy looking red coated porter rushes in and seizes Dick's luggage.

"How much?" Dick manages to gasp despite his stupor imposed by pain and medication.

"Fifty rupees," says the porter. He places the enormous back-pack on top of the suitcase containing our disassembled bike. Then he commands me in no uncertain pantomime to give him my luggage as well. But so many weeks of hassling with wannabe servants have made me stubborn. Still adorned with my own luggage, I turn my back on him and stalk off the train. When I turn around to make certain Dick and the porter are following, there is the tiny porter with the weight of an entire tandem bike balanced on top of his head and the enormous backpack piled on top of that. With one hand, he reaches up to balance his burden while gesturing wildly with the other that I have absolutely no right to carry my own luggage but must give it to him at once. In the normal course of things, insists this very small person, all four pieces of *my* luggage should *also* be piled on top of the bicycle suitcase above his head beside Dick's gigantic pack.

I shake my head with stubborn emphasis. "No! I carry my own luggage!" I insist, even though by now I have begun to understand how weird my behavior seems to an Indian peasant. I have so often puzzled at the sight of them bending very low to sweep floors and even streets with handle-less brooms. Why, I have wondered, has no one invented a broomstick? After thinking about this, I suppose that sweeping this way helps them look humble. In fact, I've noticed that they sometimes bend themselves even farther over than the length of the broom straws would require. The purpose of this could only be to exaggerate their humility, to broadcast a willingness to accept their status and conform to the norms of society.

I think about the man at the Palm Grove Hotel in Chennai, hassling me day in and day out for the privilege of shining my shoes. Surely he wouldn't do that if he knew what a nuisance it was to me. Like this man now demanding to carry my luggage, he had no idea how I pride myself in doing my own work. He had no idea how distasteful to me is the thought of being waited upon, a norm, no doubt, handed down to me from the German peasant stock that was my heritage. Maybe middle and upper class Indians think differently. Maybe if they stoop to sweep floors or polish shoes, they feel they are doing something undignified and beneath their station in life, something against the norms of society. Maybe that's why everyone in the station stares at me as I walk along beside the porter carrying my own luggage.

I have also been told that middle class Indians feel obligated to create employment by hiring others to do their work. But Dick, the manager of our funds, does not subscribe to this notion. He thinks people should instead pay taxes to support public works, garbage collection, and schools. That, he says, would create more dignified and worthwhile employment. I'm not sure who is right. Like most arguments, there are pro's and con's for either side.

Still balancing the big suitcase and, all the while, castigating me to add more tonnage, the porter leads us to the taxi stalls by climbing steep metal stairs and crossing the train yard on a long foot bridge. When he finally sets down the luggage, Dick, to my shock and dismay, actually finds within his ailing body, the energy to haggle.

"One hundred rupees," says the porter. I wonder how many times the cost would have been doubled if I had relinquished my burden to him.

"No! You said fifty," snaps Dick.

Next Dick manages to argue with the taxi driver over the cost of a ride to the hospital. Finally a policeman walks up and gets into the fray, agreeing with the taxi driver that two hundred is a fair price.

* * * *

The waiting room of the Apollo Hospital in Hyderabad, like much of the city, is a brave attempt at modernity. It is large and drafty with marble walls and a high ceiling held aloft by marble columns. At one end is a tall Christmas tree with colorful glass balls, complete with an angel on top. I have been waiting here for a long time while Dick is being x-rayed. They think he has kidney stones.

While I wait, an elderly woman comes in accompanied by three males of different generations. They are all dressed in loose peasant clothing of clean, unpressed cotton, the woman in a blue sari faded almost gray. She seems in acute distress, whimpering and clutching the left side of her head. Listening intently with my hearing aids turned up, I snatch English phrases drifting across the room . . . bleeding from the inner ear . . . emergency case . . . no money to pay . . . this is a private hospital . . . Yet Dick had been admitted without question. Because we are from a western country, no matter which one, we are assumed to be rich. In fact, by Indian standards we *are* rich. Shivering in the drafty room and wishing to be out in the sunshine on a bike, I bury my sore nostrils in a napkin swiped earlier from a chai wallah stand and watch the drama. The woman and her family are led to another counter over in the corner. Someone talks on the phone, presumably helping her find a free clinic. I imagine a little shrine to Ganesh and pray for Dick's speedy recovery, for my own devastated sinuses, but mostly for the woman who bleeds from the inner ear but has no money for treatment.

Dick comes out, sits down beside me and says, "I have three kidney stones. They're going to do ultrasound and then I will see a urologist. The doctor thinks the kidney stones will eventually pass in my urine."

"They are amazingly thorough. I wonder how much it will cost."

"Twenty-five dollars," he says, cracking his first smile of the morning.

"Twenty-five dollars? Total? For everything? The x-rays, the ultrasound, the urologist?"

"That's all. Twenty-five dollars. Well, afterwards we'll have to stop at the pharmacy stall and spend a few more rupees for a pain pill prescription."

I am astounded. In the U.S., all that would cost a fortune.

While Dick is having the ultrasound and seeing the urologist, I go out into the sunshine and walk a short way down the hillside below the hospital. There are a few mansions along the road and also some high-end apartment buildings, tropical style with arches over their balconies and red tiled roofs. Also along the same road are homeless people camped on blankets or in makeshift dwellings. One family sits in the sunshine outside their little cottage constructed of three or four discarded concrete slabs balanced haphazardly against one another. Their laundry hangs on a line strung between their extemporaneous home and another concrete slab nearby. The surrounding landscape is littered with the usual generous layers of bottles, cans, paper wrappers and plastic bags. This mixture of wealth, poverty and litter are indicative of India's freedom. They can build anything anywhere, unhampered by the design standards, building codes, and zoning ordinances of which I am so strong an advocate at home. How homesick am I for America, the land of the unfree and the home of debt slavery.

On the way back to the hospital, I stop at a drugstore stand and buy some even stronger antihistamine. After Dick is finished focusing on his own problem, he'll be angry that I didn't take advantage of this opportunity to see a doctor about some antibiotics. But I am not yet ready to give up on the immunology theory. Body and soul will heal themselves.

CHAPTER 16

Aurangabad

"Taxi, Madame!"

"You go to Ellora?"

"I take you nice hotel!"

"Brother has small business . . ."

"Professional guide service . . . perfect English"

These phrases are tossed from all sides like coins at a wishing well as I stand at dawn outside the railway station upon arriving in Aurangabad.

We had expected to attract this following. Even so, we had hoped that Mr. Chavan would be here to help us sort out which ones to trust. Dick has gone off to look for him

"We are waiting for a friend," I announce to the fray with all the confidence I can muster. Thereafter, I ignore them as though they were a flock of pigeons or crows, part of the landscape. I snatch a stolen napkin from my pocket and snort into it for emphasis.

Dick comes back calling out, "He's here! Mr. Chavan is coming!"

I turn round, and sure enough, there he is! The same dignified gentleman whose every quiet comment had been received with grave respect at the Seventh Provisional World Parliament. At the sight of his respectable demeanor, clothed in a clean white shirt and tan slacks, my encircling aviary of touts scatters to the winds.

Mr. Chavan hails a taxi, helps to stash our luggage on board, and gives an address to the driver. "The Ejin Kya Hotel is a clean and comfortable place," he tells us. "Please wait there until I come at about eleven o'clock. I am trying to set up a press conference and an opportunity for you to speak at the College. I will also speak with my son, Sunil, about the possibility of your staying at our experimental farm outside the city if you would like that. It will take a couple of hours to arrange all this."

* * * *

It is nine-thirty AM on the same warm, sunny morning of our arrival in Aurangabad. We have already checked into the Ejin Kya Hotel which provided us with two buckets of hot water. One was for doing laundry, especially my three, big, disgusting handkerchiefs and likewise soiled T-shirt. The other was to douse our weary bodies.

After washing, we walk down the long hotel driveway to this major arterial in search of breakfast. The Ejin Kya is a clean, well constructed building, but there is no concrete out here. Everything is haphazardly erected upon rock and dust.

Among the stalls we find a restaurant. Well, you might call it that. It is a stall with two formica tables in front. We seat ourselves at a table beside the busy street alive with the honks, screeches, and the roar of traffic. While we wait for the food, I drink tea and write in my diary. Dick goes over to the STD stall next door and talks with his Mom on the phone. He wishes her a Happy New Year as she sits, no doubt, by her fireplace in Washington State looking out through lead-gray curtains of rain at the Tacoma Narrows Bridge.

I make an entry in my diary.

POVERTY/PAVRATI: The most famous Hindu goddess is Pavrati, pronounced, poverty. Pavrati is the wife of the Shiva who created the universe and keeps it in existence. Legend has it that once Pavrati was having a little playful fun with Shiva and placed her hands over his eyes. Because Shiva's eyes create sunlight, all light at that moment vanished from the Universe. I presume this is to show how powerful is the goddess because of her close relationship with the god. But when I look around India, I wonder whether Pavrati might really represent its hom-

*onym, poverty. Because if poverty were revered as the head god-
dess, it could not be more prominent than it is in this most
spiritual country on earth. Poverty leaves her mark everywhere.
It cannot be evaded for a single moment. Poverty is surely the
most powerful goddess of India.*

Having written the above paragraph, I filch a few more napkins
from the holder in the center of the table and stuff them furtively
into my pocket. I feel guilty for stealing from poor people who are
so good to us, but despite much shopping, I have never been able to
buy any tissues to deal with my perpetually runny nose.

While I'm closing my diary, Mr. Chavan's business card falls
out, so I examine it carefully. It says, *Professor Sheshrao Chavan,
Bharatiya Vidya Bhavan, Chairman, Institute of World Problems, World
Citizen.*

When Dick comes back to the table, I ask, "What is 'Bharatiya
Vidya Bhavan'?"

"I'm not sure, but I think it is a sort of liberal religious and
cultural organization. They are into serving humanity, making
the world a better place."

"Maybe Mr. Chavan is a real kindred spirit," I say.

"I believe so," says Dick. "We'll soon find out. I just phoned
him. He's bringing his son to meet us at eleven o'clock."

* * * *

We don't have to sit with our guests on the edge of the bed this
time. Our room at the Ejin Kya has its own little settee and coffee
table. Mr. Chavan and his son, Sunil, sit across from me and Dick
in separate comfortable chairs. They fill us in on the wonders they
have achieved in the course of a few hours. "There will be a press
conference at our offices and, on the same day, you will speak to an
assembly of students at the College." Mr. Chavan smiles softly with
a far off look in his eye almost as though, strangely enough, this is a
dream coming true for him more than us. He is thin and muscular
with a dark face framed in gold-rimmed spectacles and a fluffy crop
of white hair. Although his voice is deep and resonant, he lets it rise
to a characteristically Indian high pitch and volume as he adds, "Everyone is eager to meet you."

"When? Today?" I ask, hoping our laundry will be dry in time.

"Oh, no," says Sunil. "We have scheduled everything for Monday." Sunil's eyes radiate that gentle kindness, characteristic of so many Indian faces. He is larger and a little more filled out than his father. "Today is Friday, and we are heading into the weekend. Nothing could be arranged for today. We are sorry. Are you in a hurry to leave Aurangabad?"

Dick says, "I wonder what we will do in the meantime." I imagine his mathematical mind calculating the distance and possible road conditions between here and Bombay where we are scheduled to be in two weeks.

"There is much to do in Aurangabad," says Mr. Chavan. "You must visit the Ellora Caves and Ajanta Caves. These are some of India's most cherished antiquities."

"And you must spend time visiting with us at the farm and learn about sustainable agriculture," says Sunil.

"Besides that, we will strategize how to create a global parliament for the planet earth," says Mr. Chavan.

"And Mona must rest to get well. She seems to have a bad cold," observes Sunil.

"Wow! What a program!" says Dick.

"Can we do all that between now and Monday?" I ask.

"No! You must stay longer," says Sunil. Then he turns to his father and says something in Hindi. Mr. Chavan replies. They smile and nod to one another.

Mr. Chavan says, "How long will it take to put your bicycle together?"

"A couple of hours," says Dick.

"Then you must assemble the bicycle and ride out to the farmhouse this afternoon."

* * * *

After the Chavans leave, Dick and I hug and congratulate one another for the good luck we are having. Then Dick opens the big suitcase and starts to work. He carefully spreads out the dozens of little metal parts over the floor. He is getting pretty good at this jigsaw puzzle. While he works, I gather up the laundry (which is already mostly dry) and pack our things. After packing, I lie down in a patch of sun shining through the window onto the bed and sleep off my heavy dose of antihistamine.

When Dick wakes me up, our beautiful blue double cycle is parked against the wall beside the bed. The trailer is all packed with our banner draped over the top. "It's time to go," he says.

Feeling a little better after my nap, I am eager to get on the road. Besides, the most important element of the immunology theory is the exercise. Theoretically, the reason I'm sick is because I have had so little exercise this week what with attending meetings and riding trains.

The hotel staff stare in wide-eyed wonder when we wheel our big contraption, the likes of which they have never imagined, into their lobby. From whence did it come? We didn't have it when we checked in. We act as though materializing large exotic vehicles out of thin air is standard ordinary procedure, which for us, it is.

As the crowds gather outside the hotel, Dick casually attaches the trailer while, I hold the bike upright. We mount up, and we're off. The crowd cheers, hoots, and waves goodbye. All along the street, people shout at us in Hindi. I have no idea what they are saying. I hope it's good.

Following Mr. Chavan's directions, we head out of town and wend our way toward the fabled "farmhouse." I peer anxiously over Dick's shoulder at the white sun sphere sinking lower into the haze up ahead.

Shortly after we pass the city limits, the chain falls off our bike, so we have to stop. I hold the rear wheel aloft while Dick puts the chain back on and turns the crank to thread the long delicate strand of metal linkages through all its gears. While crossing a bridge (which wasn't supposed to be there according to the map) we conclude that we passed our turn and have to go back.

We have barely corrected our course, before the chain falls off again. "I'll have to fine-tune this thing tomorrow," Dick grumbles as I lift the rear wheel for him to replace the chain again.

After making one more wrong turn and doubling back again, we are finally on the right road. The massive "Tower of the Moon" rising over the medieval, walled fortress of Daulatabad crowns the hillside on our right. Our guidebook says this formidably fortified compound served as headquarters of the powerful Yadava rulers. In the 13th century, Mohammed bin Tughlak, the Sultan of Delhi, made it his capital. A pale yolk of sun now peers through the curtain of haze hanging over the Deccan plateau. Time is short today. We will stop and look at the fortress another time.

It is almost dusk when we spot Sunil waiting with a motorcycle at a road junction. He waves in cheerful greeting and leads us up a dusty road with a few remnants of patchy, broken pavement. He drives as slowly as the machine will allow, so we can follow with the bike. He has to stop frequently and wait for us.

After turning into the Chavan's driveway, we ride through a mini-forest of little plants growing in white plastic bags. They are the same ugly plastic bag pollutants we have seen strewn across the face of India. How reassuring it is to see so many put to good use as planting pots!

Dominating the scene in almost comical contrast with the size of the little plants is the farmhouse, a gray stone structure with massive pillars, wide verandas, and a few slits for windows high in the walls. We follow the curve of the stone porch around to the front and discover Mr. Chavan seated peacefully in the advancing twilight reading a book. He is dwarfed by four massive ionic columns across the front of the house.

We get off the bike and lean it up against the foundation, which is vastly different from any building we have yet seen in India or anywhere else. We climb several stone steps to the porch which is an extension of the main floor.

We follow Mr. Chavan and his son through the heavy front door into the main room. The walls are at least two feet thick and twenty feet high. Supporting the roof are four rows of heavy, exposed beams. Several doors open from the main room into adjoining rooms. There appear to be no hallways in the entire house. All rooms lead off this central living area. The most prominent piece of furniture is a big oval conference table flanked by chalk boards and easels. Perhaps this was once a British country house now converted to the useful and democratic purpose of teaching sustainable agriculture.

Mr. Chavan leads us to one of the adjoining rooms which is to be our bedroom. This space alone is as large as entire middle class Indian apartments we have seen. The walls appear to have been neatly white-washed long ago, and the paint has aged gracefully. There are several windows crowned with arched pains of frosted glass. Best of all, this bedroom has its own bathroom with a sit-down toilet. Mr. Chavan encourages us to "freshen up," this time fortunately with the help of a little warm water, and come out onto the porch for tea.

The tea is served on a small portable table. The servant, or so he must be, is a young man who is introduced as "Ganesh." He has handsome classic Indian features and a sweet, gentle demeanor. After he has served our tea, I see him scurrying about among the plants with a watering can.

"What is growing in the little white bags?" I ask Mr. Chavan.

"Tomatoes, guavas, mangos, many foods will grow this way," he says. "It is an experiment. Appropriate technology."

"How so?"

"With this system, a farmer needs only one acre of land to earn the annual income that now requires five acres. In fact, a family can grow most of its food using only a roof garden."

"Cool! Is this hydroponic gardening?" I ask.

"Oh, no chemicals," Mr. Chavan shudders. "All natural fertilizers. After we finish our tea, I'll take you on a tour of the farm. But now I would like to know what you thought of the meeting in Chennai."

I shrug. "A good exercise, I suppose. And very good people. Their hearts are in the right place."

Mr. Chavan smiles in a sort of recognition reflex. "That meeting accomplished very little," he says. "What good does it do to pass laws that no one will obey? If you want a world parliament, you have to organize."

"It's difficult to organize the world," says Dick.

"And what will you accomplish by bicycling around the world?" asks Mr. Chavan.

"If nothing else, we will educate ourselves. But maybe we will cause people who have never heard of global democracy to think about it. There will never be a world parliament if people don't think about it," I say.

Mr. Chavan grimaces. "If you want a world parliament, you have to promote it."

Dick says, "That's why we came to India. We're going to the World Social Forum. Among the thousands of people, there will be eighteen different groups promoting global democracy. We hope to build a global umbrella organization."

"Our mission is promotion among the people," I say. "But we are promoting the ideas of international law experts Richard Falk and Andrew Strauss. They say the parliament could be started by as few as twenty to thirty countries signing onto a treaty. As the parliament becomes effective, it will gain publicity. Then people from other countries will pressure their governments to sign on."

Mr. Chavan nods enthusiastically. Then he says, "If you want to organize, you must learn from Gandhi. Gandhi won India's independence from Britain and gave birth to a democratic nation. That was a tremendous accomplishment. The way he did it was to identify a few people he could trust, people who were very committed and would work for the cause. We need to identify the twenty countries that will likely sign the treaty. Then we find at least two people in each country who will be committed."

"Will you help?" I ask. I notice his switch from *you* to *we* in the last sentences.

"I will be one of the two people in India," he says.

Perhaps out of excitement or gratitude about Mr. Chavan's commitment or perhaps because a waft of evening breeze carries the wrong combination of pollen and dust, I respond with a violent sneeze.

Dick says, "It's starting to get dark. Will you show us your plants this evening?"

"Yes. Let's bring our tea along so it won't get cold."

In the gathering dusk, we walk past hundreds of carefully measured rows of plastic bags. Most of the small plants are adorned with little balls of fruit in various stages of ripening.

"Each plant requires two liters of water per week," says Mr. Chavan. "And the plants are fed compost made of food scraps from the table or food stuffs thrown away at the market." He shows us a large compost bin off to one side. "If we add micro-organisms, the compost matures in just a few weeks."

"Sounds good," I say, but I wonder whether this system is really all that new. It seems quite simple, almost obvious.

As if he has read my mind, Mr. Chavan says, "With this system, a farmer who earns 30,000 rupees per year can now earn 100,000 rupees. We have tested this."

"That's remarkable!" Some things that seem simple and obvious are not always recognized until someone points them out.

"With this system, we can popularize the idea of a world parliament among the people."

My nose emits an intense fit of wheezing.

Dick says, "We applaud what you are doing, Mr. Chavan. But what is the connection between agricultural technology and world parliament?"

"If you triple peoples' incomes and bring them out of poverty, they will think you are a god. They will be receptive to anything else you are promoting. People followed Gandhi, not as much for his political beliefs as for his ability to show them how to live. You can't win over the people unless you connect with their concerns."

"But there are so many people in so many different countries. They all have different concerns. How can you connect with all of them?" I sniffle.

"They all want to care for their families. That is their foremost concern. But my concern is for you now. Perhaps the air out here is aggravating your condition. Besides, it is dark. We should continue our conversation inside. Ganesh has gone home, but Sunil will serve us dinner."

* * * *

Dick and I have the eating customs down pat. Before dinner we go into the bathroom and washed our hands thoroughly. We don't necessarily expect utensils or napkins, nor do we expect anyone to eat with us.

Mr. Chavan invites us to join him at the end of his big conference table, and, to our delight, he does eat with us. Sunil, however, does not. Instead, he goes and comes from the kitchen relentlessly offering us more food. I have very little appetite, probably because of the antihistamine, so I soon feel overfed.

"What is your profession? What kind of work do you do?" I ask Sunil when, to my relief, he finally sits down to watch us eat.

Mr. Chavan speaks for him. "Sunil is in charge of a program in several Aurangabad high schools. Hundreds of students are involved."

"We organize the students into what we call *clean brigades*," says Sunil.

"Oh!" I brighten with intense interest, having indulged myself in grandiose fantasies about organizing millions of people all over the country to join in neighborhood clean-ups and pick up all the garbage of India.

"What do they clean?" I ask. I picture the students running around town picking up garbage and putting "Don't litter" signs on trash cans.

"They do many things," he says. "They test soil samples, air samples, water samples. They plant city gardens on rooftops using our system. They compost food wastes, many things."

"What if their tests find pollutants?"

"They write letters to the editor and complain to the city departments in charge of that."

"Do they pick up garbage?"

Sunil gives me a puzzled look. "Sometimes. But that isn't the main focus of a clean brigade. The idea is to *keep* things clean. In a truly sustainable world, there would be no waste."

Now I am confused. I wonder how they *keep* things clean unless they *get* them clean first.

Mr. Chavan says, "If the students were to pick up all the trash, where would you have them put it?"

"In the garbage can?"

"Where would it go from there?"

"To a land-fill?" I am starting to get the point. The clean brigade's mission is not to make the city look pretty so it won't be an eyesore for tourists. The clean brigade tries to improve the health of the environment and therefore the people. I recall Mr. Chavan's earlier comment, "They will think you are a god."

* * * *

Today is Monday morning, January fifth. Fortunately, I feel much better. Today is a workday. We will ride the bike back into

Aurangabad for a press conference and speak at the college. At the moment, I am sitting here on the back porch of the farmhouse in the sunshine reflecting upon an unforgettable weekend and writing an entry in my diary.

> *On Saturday Dick and I rode the bike to the Ellora Caves. The ride, sans trailer, was a delight. We pedaled through hilly country that reminded us of Eastern Oregon, especially where the road wound up through valleys with steep brown hills rimmed in layers of sedimentary rock. On the way, we saw, for the first time, real Indian bicycle tourists. They were not rigged out with panniers and expensive gear. Instead, they rode simple black one-speed bikes with duffel bags strapped to their luggage racks.*
>
> *The cave temples must truly be among the world's top wonders, scores of them carved into one stone monolith. Ornate temples and domes crown its peak. Enormous rooms with colonnades proceed downward from that in all directions.*
>
> *Three religions were represented, Buddhism, Hinduism, and Jainism. The Buddhist shrines were peaceful and contemplative, but even they are almost inevitably flanked by voluptuous goddesses with gracefully curved hips and generous bosoms, larger than life. The Hindu temples are busy and charged with energy. Instead of the Buddha, sitting quietly and meditating, the Hindu temples depicte active myths and stories.*
>
> *The best part for me was to walk into a temple past pillars and carvings and find a gentle Buddha face catching light that filtered in through the darkness. To think he had been sitting in meditation since perhaps the 7th century AD! Feeling as though I was in the womb of Mother Earth, I would rest peacefully gazing at a statue while Dick scurried about reading the guidebook, making sure not to miss anything. My body, after all, was fighting off a monstrous infection.*

All I did yesterday was lie here on the porch in the sunshine. That may be why I feel better. I don't know for sure that I have it licked yet, but at least I can function. I didn't even have to take any antihistamines this morning.

Mr. Chavan comes out and says it's time to leave for the press conference. I am ready for anything.

* * * *

Following in the wake of Sunil and Mr. Chavan in their car, we slowly make headway through the turmoil of traffic. They turn right into a middle class residential neighborhood of well-maintained concrete block houses. We stop in front of a two-story building with a courtyard. Attached to the garden wall is a simple, well-designed sign that reads, *Bharatiya Vidya Bhavan.*

Beyond the entrance, a wide hallway opens into a conference room with rows of plastic molded chairs, the like of which there must be millions in India. Mr. Chavan leads us to a table up front which has been equipped with a microphone. People filling in the chairs appear to be professional and well off, women in smart crisp saris, men in suits and ties. Mr. Chavan introduces them as doctor of this or professor that. Most are microbiologists and environmental scientists. The scene is in some vague way reminiscent of the police station in Bayana. The plastic chairs are identical to those, manufactured no doubt from the same mold. Just as in Bayana, we are sitting in front of an audience very near the microphone. Only this time I gather, we *are* "It." There is no police chief or other official waiting to make a speech and field the questions. But this audience seems more sophisticated. I utter a prayer of gratitude to Ganesh and the Universe that on this day I have not yet felt the trace of a sniffle, let alone a sneeze.

When the reporter shows up, I am very much at ease. By now I have spoken with several Indian reporters, and they have all had a knack for empathy to rival the best trained psychotherapists. Besides, the questions are always the same:

"What is the Global Peoples Assembly Movement?"

"How many people are there in the movement?"

They want to know our political views, what we think of the war, what we like and don't like about India.

The conference lasts for more than an hour with people from the audience also asking questions. Mr. Chavan asks, "Mona, what would you like to say to the women of India?"

"How much I admire their strength," I say. "I have seen them carry bowls of rocks on their heads in limestone quarries and road crews. I have seen them working in the fields. I also admire the way they have produced great leaders like Indira Gandhi, Vandana Shiva, Arundati Roy. The women of India do the work."

"What advise would you give them?" persists Mr. Chavan.

"Ride bicycles," I say.

Everyone laughs.

"Why should they ride bicycles?"

"It gives one a sense of freedom."

"I suppose it's difficult to ride a bicycle while wearing a sari," says Mr. Chavan.

"It can be done. I saw two women doing that in Gangaphur." I say. "But I have to admit, I would not want to try it." I had hoped that comment would get a laugh, but it didn't.

After the press conference two boys from the college meet us outside on bicycles. They are dressed in precision-creased blue slacks and flawless white shirts with ties. They lead us to the college where a large gathering of young people stands outside waiting to welcome us. The boys are all dressed like our two cycling guides and the girls wear identical soft blue saris with white dupattas. The Head Master shows up with several other faculty members. They present us with bouquets of flowers and award us with plaques. I don't know what we have done to deserve all this. In India honors are bestowed with generous abandon. But we are ready to earn some of this by delivering our Bike for Global Democracy stump speeches with more aplomb than ever before. I begin by saying "You, the young people of India, are the world's great hope. If you make sure India is one of the first countries to sign onto a treaty starting a world parliament, that will be the greatest single event in history. India is after all the largest and perhaps the most credible democracy on the planet."

CHAPTER 17

Birthday Party

We leave the Aurangabad farm on the morning of January 7. Mr. Chavan, Sunil, and Ganesh gather at the end of their driveway clearing surrounded by their miniature vegetable plantation. In the background looms their impressive gray stone farmhouse.

Every nerve in my body is shriveled up from endorphin withdrawal, and positively aches to be *on the road again,* but it still hurts to say goodbye to these gentle souls who have treated us so well. Another newfound family left behind. But at least we face the prospect of seeing Mr. Chavan again as he has promised to show up at the World Social Forum in Mumbai and to help organize a global democracy coalition.

Once clear of the rutted gravel roads leading away from the farmhouse, we are on relatively smooth straight pavement skimming past stubble fields from a variety of crops, cotton, wheat, rice, and some more exotic ones we cannot name. These flat fields, brown and fallow in the off-season, wait patiently for summer monsoons to quench their thirst and bring them back to life. These fields call to mind off-season visits to the monotonous southern Illinois country where my mother grew up, except those farms had been brown from cold, not drought, in winter. This day is balmy as springtime in Illinois, and the thick dusty air burns my nostrils like Illinois summer.

I reach in my pocket for a strong dose of antihistamine and swallow it down with a couple sips from my water bottle. Then I close my eyes and drift into the aerobic meditation which I have perfected with so much cycling. Now I picture a Buddha statue, way back in the Ellora Caves. I imagine that my mind is his, a psyche suspended in repose for the last 2500 years, like the spirit of a California redwood forever poised in silent watchfulness of the eternal NOW.

An all too familiar thud, thud, under my tail bone brings me out of the trance. I open my eyes and look out at the world. To our great fortune, today's first flat tire has occurred in front of a restaurant way out in the countryside. Several outdoor tables adorn a clean paved surface in front.

I glance at my watch. It is nearly noon, but the place seems almost deserted except for a dough-boy shaped man with intelligent dark eyes who stands in front gesturing for us to come into the yard.

"We can change the tire and then have lunch," says Dick. "This must be one of those family style restaurants set up for the tourist buses going to Ajanta and Ellora."

While Dick changes the tire, the proprietor and two wiry fellows, probably his assistants, come out to watch. I show them our most recent picture and newspaper article from Aurangabad. The inscrutable symbols in which it is written are, I'm told, the local language, Marathi.

The proprietor takes the article and reads it carefully. Then he chatters to the others.

They smile, nod, and make approving noises. "Good cause," says the proprietor and hands me back the article.

When we sit down at one of the tables, the proprietor gives us English menus and waits with pad and pencil to take our orders. Since that unforgettable meal in our grungy *lodging* in Susner, I have always known what to order. "Green Salad." Yes, here it is. I point to the item on the menu.

"Ah, yes, green salad." The man nods, smiles, and writes on his pad.

But Dick chimes in, "What do you want in your salad?"

I shrug. "The usual. Tomatoes, carrots, radishes, beets."

"You don't want any onions do you?" He must have noticed that previously I have eaten everything else and left the onion slices on my plate. I like onions, but I would normally pad them between a garden burger and a bun or chop them up in a stir fry. I can't handle several slices of raw onion unmitigated by nothing more than a squeeze of lime.

"No," I say. "I really don't want onions."

"Then maybe you should tell him you don't want onions, so they won't be wasted."

Something tells me to not to upset the communication boat, but to please Dick, I look at the waiter and say, "Green salad but no onions."

The man wrinkles his brow. His head wobbles from side to side, then he shakes it emphatically. "No have," he says.

"Do you have green salad?" I ask.

"Yes."

"I'll have green salad," I repeat without qualification.

But Dick takes a piece of paper out of his pocket and writes, "Green Salad." Below that, he writes, "No onions." Below that he makes a list, "Carrots, tomatoes, radishes."

"What else do you want?" he asks.

"Cucumbers, beets, and a lime on top."

Dick adds cucumbers and beets to the list, then shows it to the man. "She wants a salad with carrots, tomatoes, cucumbers, beets but no onions," he says. Fortunately he doesn't try to make this even more complicated by trying to insert a few words of the native language. He is at a loss for that now. We have come into Marathi country where his dozen or so Hindi phrases are useless.

The man looks at Dick's message and shakes his head several times. Then he goes back to the kitchen and brings out his two helpers. They all look at the paper and chatter for awhile in Marathi. Finally they shake their heads in unison like a dancing chorus line.

The proprietor hands me back the paper. "No have," he says and poises the pencil over his pad as if waiting for me to order something else.

Exasperated, I snatch Dick's paper, circle the phrase, "Green Salad," and draw two arrows pointing to the circle. Then I scribble out all the other words, carrots, tomatoes, etc. and hand the paper back to the man. "Do you have Green Salad?" I ask pointing to the words.

The man smiles relief and nods several times. "Yes, yes. Green Salad," he assures me.

When my plate arrives, it contains the usual selection of vegetables including a generous helping of sliced raw onions.

"It's best not to try and get too specific," I advise Dick. "If you try to get exactly what you want, you may not get anything at all."

"It's a pity to waste all those onions," he moans. "But I wonder why they call it 'Green Salad.' It isn't green."

"Maybe green means raw to them," I suggest. "Meanings are in people, not in words."

When the proprietor comes to take our plates away, Dick takes out his wallet and asks, "What cost?"

The proprietor shakes his head. "No cost," he says. "Good cause."

Even though this is not the first time we have been overwhelmed by the generosity of Indian people, we are, as always, dumbfounded. Hugging people is not permissible, so we bow several times with prayer hands forward. "Thank you. Thank you. Namaste!" we repeat several times.

* * * *

The sun sets over the village of Nandgaon on our first day out of Aurangabad. Standing nude beside the shower/laundry bucket of cold water, I watch the sun from a paneless bathroom window no larger than my head. Visible through the curtain of air pollution, the sun drops below the roof of a building and disappears, taking with it the last rays of light I was using for laundry detail.

The surface of the cold water shimmers in the in the increasing darkness as I work tactilely with a tiny sliver of hand soap trying to wash my three slimey handkerchiefs. The surrounding tile toilet stall is larger than usual but is also covered with the normal layer of greasy film. The only blessing is that the air is warm. If this climate were cold as Washington State, all else being equal, there would be no hope of my surviving this trip.

It seems impossible that we left Aurangabad only this morning.

Surely it has been eons since our free lunch today at the roadside restaurant. Time moves slowly during travel, and we exist in the all too present moment that is India.

It must have been about mid-afternoon when Dick had stopped to study the map. Mr. Chavan had advised us to go to Shirdi tonight, insisting we should see the shrine to Sai Baba, a legendary modern day saint. He had assured us there would be plenty of lodging in Shirdi.

On hindsight, we should have taken his advice. But the map showed the road to Shirdi as a secondary road, so we decided to come to Nandgaon instead, believing a primary road would be smoother and therefore easier on our tires. However, the road to Nangoan had gotten worse from that point on. Large segments of sparse and narrow blacktop were completely missing. We had experienced two more flats before arriving in this very small village. Then it was only by luck that a young man rescued us from a hassling crowd and brought us to this government guest house for the night.

I am still wringing out handkerchiefs and underwear when Dick pokes his head in through the door. "How are you feeling?" he asks.

"Alright," I say. No need to mention that my nose is very sore, and I can't breath.

"We are invited to dinner with some folks in the building next door. The guy speaks English. He's a local official from the regional water department. They seem like nice people."

"Okay, I'll be along in a minute." A banana would have squelched my hunger, but I was not about to miss an opportunity to interact with the people. After all, I would probably never be back to Nandgaon again.

* * * *

When I come out of our building into the surrounding darkness, it is easy to tell where to go. This government guest house consists of a compound of small buildings scattered at random over a few acres of dusty earth and surrounded by a wrought iron fence. A dim light shines from within the building next door. I can see silhouettes of people and hear conversation and laughter.

Inside, several respectable looking men in clean western style clothing sit in a circle of upholstered chairs around a candlelit coffee table. They all stand to greet me and shake my hand as Dick introduces me. A handsome man name Pramid Patil offers me a chair. In the dim light, I can see this cabin is much cheerier than ours. The walls are freshly painted a sunny shade of yellow, and the beds are covered with matching yellow spreads trimmed with colorful geometric patterns. Pramid introduces two of his companions as *block leaders,* which he defines as some sort of elective office.

"How large is a block?" I ask picturing what I think of as a city block in the U.S.

"Blocks vary in size," Pramid explains. "They may take in as many as two or three towns and villages."

I assume that the *block leaders* are not as comfortable with English as Pramid, who intermittently speaks Marathi to them on the side, presumably translating. There is, however, an even better English speaker here named Saujiv Damne. Pramid and Mr. Damne do most of the talking, and we soon learn that Mr. Damne is the owner of a scientific laboratory as well as a reporter for the local newspaper. As soon as I am seated, he moves his chair over next to mine. "Your husband tells me you have published a book," he says. "Have you brought copies with you?"

"No. Books are too heavy to carry on the bicycle. But if you give me your address, I'll send you one later."

"Tell me all about your book. I would like to know the whole story."

"Well, the title is *Alien Child.* It is about a woman named Wella. She comes from a planet called Gallata where women run the government and there is no word for war in any language."

A murmur of Marathi swells the room as Pramid translates. "No war!" says Pramid. "That might not be so if women control the government." Everyone laughs.

"But let her tell the story," insists Mr. Damne.

"So this woman comes to earth. She is taking part in a genetic study. She has to conceive a child by an earth human."

A ripple of oh's and ah's spreads through the small audience as if they are imagining the conception scene.

"So she has the child. But the child doesn't know she is half-alien. She is adopted and raised by an earth family. But she has psychic abilities which she develops on her own throughout childhood. When she grows up, she uses those psychic abilities to assist a movement toward a just, democratic, world government."

"Oooh! That is a wonderful book!" says Mr. Damne. "It is remarkable how your story reminds me of a book my father wrote. Like you, my father had another career serving humanity. He is a physician, but he writes science fiction for a hobby."

"I would like to read your father's book," I say. "Can you tell us the story?"

"In my father's book, people leave planet earth to travel to distant places in the universe."

"Like in the American televisions series," says one of the *block leaders*.

"Yes, like *Star Trek*," says Dick.

"But this is a very different story," says Mr. Damne. "In my father's book, these people are able to clone themselves, only with a special technique using a part of the brain that stores memories. So the clones have the same memories as the originals."

"What a wonderful idea!" I say. "In that case, it would be almost as if they were the same people, almost as if they were immortal."

"Yes, but that isn't the main point. Eventually these people return to earth and find that mankind has destroyed itself."

"How sad," says one of the *block leaders*.

"Sad, but very likely," says the other.

"But then the people begin life anew in the way of nonviolence and sustainability," says Mr. Damne.

Dick says, "Those are both lovely stories, but I hope we can achieve global democracy and a just, sustainable world without extraterrestrial interventions."

Pramid says, "Will you make the world just and sustainable by bicycling around it in your old age telling people about global democracy?"

"No," says Dick. "But we want to make people think about global democracy. The more people think about it, the more likely it is to happen. We are the product of our thoughts."

Mr. Damne says, "It is a wonderful thing that you can bicycle around the world at your age. How old are you?"

Dick says, "I am fifty-seven. My wife is sixty-four."

More ooh's and aah's ripple about the circle while I remember something. "Actually, tomorrow is my birthday. I will be sixty-*five*."

"Truly?" says Pramid. "Tomorrow is your birthday and you will be sixty-five years old?"

This creates a stir in the room as various side conversations erupt in Marathi. The Marathi asides continue for quite awhile as food is brought in, and Dick and I are offered plates of chapatis, lentils, and rice. While we are munching, Pramid says to Dick. "What is your schedule tomorrow? Can you remain in Nandgaon until noon? We have a small function we would like you to attend. We would also like to take you on a tour of the Jain temple here in the village."

"That sounds great!" says Dick. "Our plan was to reach Manmad by tomorrow evening, but that is only forty kilometers from here. I'm sure we can make that even if the roads are bad."

"Fine with me," I say. Actually, I wouldn't mind staying in Nandgaon even longer than that. The conversation has been good and the people friendly.

* * * *

It is the morning of January 8, 2004, my sixty-fifth birthday. I sit on the stoop in the sunshine outside our building at the Nandgaon government guest house writing in my diary. Dick kneels on the ground a few feet away repairing inner tubes. At first, we don't notice the three smiling elders until they are just a few feet away, standing erect with poise and perfect posture. Trailing in their wake is a younger man in a tan windbreaker with a large camera hanging from his shoulder by a strap.

One of the three is dressed in a golden Nehru suit, the other two in white western style suits, spotlessly clean and pressed. There is a dignity and decorum in their manner like that of government officials attending a state ceremony. However, their white silk shirt collars open at the neck without ties tend to soften the formality of their appearance, so Dick and I don't feel out of place in our bicycling attire of khaki pants and T-shirts. They begin with introductions, clichés of greeting and welcoming, but their beautiful names fly over my head like chortling finches, never lighting perceptibly upon my ear drums, let alone my memory. "We are honored that you have come to Nandgaon and will celebrate your sixty-fifth birth-day with us," says the tallest, most dignified looking gentleman in the Nehru suit.

The shortest and frailest looking one reads a poem he wrote only this morning, just for this occasion. After the poem, the taller man presents me with a pretty scarf and a bouquet of flowers. Then we stand in a row to have our pictures taken. Having lived the first sixty-five years as an ordinary person, a school girl, then a mom and a modestly paid civil servant, I have never felt so honored in my life. I assume that was the *function* to which Pramid had referred. But they beckon us to follow. There is more to come. "We will go to the most ancient street of our village now and tour the temple," says the taller man.

We parade down hill and then turn into a narrow street wind-ing sharply up another hill. This must have been the main street of Nandgaon for centuries. In layout and design, it is much like medi-eval streets of Europe with the facades of houses leaning out over the shops. But here the shops are stalls with counters crossing their fronts and open to the air like so many other Indian stores. The houses above these stores are made of random materials, wood, brick, and stone. They appear to have been constructed directly from the builders' imaginations with no need for the superfluous interven-tion of a draftsman. Each of the three gentlemen points out this own house as we parade up the street, now joined by more and more people.

When we arrive at the Jain temple, most of our followers wait outside while a small group of elders takes us on the tour. Like other Jain temples we have visited, the walls are lavishly adorned with mirror mosaics, colorful gems, and carvings. It feels like we are in-side a giant jewelry box.

In stark contrast with the rest of the décor, however, is one wall hung with life-sized photographs of nude, elderly men seated in the lotus position. The tall gentleman explains that these are former swamis of the temple, going back several generations. "In the Jain religion," he says, "A holy man wears nothing. He owns nothing, eats very little. This is to teach us that the spirit is everything. Mat-ter is nothing."

Next we file up a stone staircase to the roof where we sit for group photos among ornately carved white pillars and cupolas of the temple. These roof structures look like a mammoth display of fanciful cake decorations laid out for a contest showing by skilled pastry chefs. At first thought, there seems to be a contradiction between this lush décor and the Jain notion of simplicity that, "spirit is everything." But, on second thought, these airy adornments lead the mind away from mundane concerns into the realm of spirit.

After the temple tour, we proceed across the street and climb a narrow staircase over a drug store. At the top of the stairs stands Saujiv Damne with his wife, father, and mother in their living room. It is a fairly large room by the standards of Indian homes, perhaps the size of an average American living room.

We file in with the elders and sit down on the chairs followed by a steady stream of villagers. After the chairs are filled, a standing circle forms behind them. People also line the stairway. Through the open window in front, we can see that the street below is full of people looking up, waving and smiling. This is turning out to be,

Posing with elders on the roof of the Jain Temple in Nandgaon.

by far, the biggest birthday party of my life. I suppose this must be the gods way of making it up to me for so many birthdays that have gone unnoticed. Being born exactly two weeks after Christmas and one week after New Years Day guaranteed me an anticlimactic birthday. Everyone is tired of celebrating by January 8th.

The Mrs. Damnes pass around trays of tea glasses and sweets. The elder Mrs. Damne comes over to me and places a small piece of cake in my mouth as the photographer takes our picture. The elders make more speeches about how honored they are by our visit, as the younger Mr. Damne translates everything into Marathi. The older, Dr. Damne presents more gifts, another silk scarf and a tiny figurine of Ganesh.

Next Pramid, who is standing at the edge of the circle, coaches me saying, "Now Mona will please make a speech. Tell everyone about your family. That is what Indian people want to know. They want to know how old are your children, what is their line of work, whether they are happy."

"Yes, always Indian people want to know these things," agrees the oldest, sweetest man who had written the poem. This comes as no surprise. We have been asked these same questions over and over again on this trip. I tell them my children are in their middle thirties. My daughter is a successful information technology manager for a biotech firm in Boston; my son manages a ski mountaineering shop in Seattle. I tell them my children are happy, but I am not yet, nor soon to be, if ever, a grandmother. Some smile, others breathe pitying sighs or shake their heads as this shocking information is translated.

After the speeches, the rest of the guests wait out in the street while the village elders and the Damne family file with us up into Dr. Damne's roof garden. More pictures are taken amidst a miniature tropical jungle of mango trees, tomatoes plants, birds of paradise, ferns, and roses.

When we file back out into the street full of well wishers, the crowd gives way and ushers two teenaged girls up front, each to present me with a small plump rose. These are not the sterile professional variety of roses with regulation length stems you might purchase near the checkout counter at an American supermarket. There is a rustic quality about them as though they may have been clipped from a wild bush or family garden.

Looking into the faces of these two beautiful children, it crosses my mind that, of all the snapshots and photos of the trip, this is the one I will cherish. I don't have them on film unfortunately, but I have them in memory. The details of this memory will fade but its essence will always be with me. The essence is not their pretty flowered print dresses trimmed in eyelet and ruffles, their colorful silk scarves tied about their heads. It is not even their exquisite dark eyes, so full of love for life, as embodied in a strange old woman. It is the way love pours out from these girls and from their community openly and freely to a stranger. This must be the true meaning of generosity, a lesson gratefully learned by taking a wrong road.

CHAPTER 18

Pilgrims on the Road to Bombay

Much of the time since leaving Monmad we have been cycling on the primary road that will take us the rest of the way to Bombay. Mercifully, on this relatively smooth pavement, we have averaged no more than one flat tire each day. We never received any replacements from Oregon, but we now have high hopes that our multiple-patched inner tubes will make it through the last few days of our journey.

In Nasik, I finally gave up on the immunology theory and saw a doctor who prescribed antibiotics for my sinus infection. The pain is mostly gone now, but I still have a trace of the sniffles. I keep the three big colorful handkerchiefs tied to the handle bars, and they flap like banners before my eyes as we ride along. Beyond them, I can see a brown camel hump of a hill rising out of a barren plane into the pale yellow sky.

Beside the road marches a stalwart procession of pilgrims wearing red bandanas around their necks. There must be hundreds in this crew. Red scarves have shown up in several groupings throughout the day. We don't know for sure where these hikers are going or why, but we are told many are headed for Shirdi to visit the shrine to Sai Baba, a modern day saint who

died in 1918. We pass a gaggle of women pilgrims all wearing
white saris. They carry white cloth bundles hung from sticks flung
over their shoulders. Farther down, three completely nude men,
possibly Jain holy men, trip briskly and unabashedly along in plain
view of the highway.

The pilgrimage phenomenon is as intriguing to us as much of
the vast panorama of Indian spiritual life. Pilgrimage is a very popular notion. In fact, we're told it's a religious obligation to undertake
a pilgrimage now and then, a necessary aspect of one's spiritual development.

Perhaps some innate pilgrimage tendency grows perennially in
human nature, resurrecting itself even in the supposedly secular
societies of America. There are obvious similarities, for example,
between these pilgrimages and people signing up for volksmarches
and organized bike rides in the States. In fact, the folks with the red
bandanas have a sag wagon much like the Cascade Bicycle Club
provides for its annual Seattle to Portland bike ride.

Perhaps, from an Indian perspective, Dick and I are ourselves
on a pilgrimage. There is something spiritual about what we are

Dick poses with the bike before an old road shrine.

doing even though we have never labeled it as such. I can feel our souls growing and our spirits unfolding on this trip. Maybe that's why people are so good to us. To them, we are pilgrims traveling about the world under our own steam searching for god. I may be starting to understand Gandhi's definition of humility. *The seeker after truth must become humbler than dust.* Humility must include a willingness to let the *universe* be in control when things don't turn out as one might hope. None of our memorable experiences on this trip were planned. We have let the gods provide and whatever it was, no matter how shabby or unsanitary, turned out to be a thing of beauty.

The road starts to climb a hillside wooded with lightly foliated trees and sparse undergrowth. The air feels a little fresher here. I feel a sense of exhilaration as my nostrils manage to suck a tiny jet of oxygen up through a passageway that had long since atrophied and given up hope of ever breathing again.

We stop by a makeshift roadside restaurant, the usual rough cut poles tied to sheets of blackened tin roofing. This appears to be an Indian version of a truck stop. Besides the usual assortment of motorcycles, a number of gaily painted trucks are parked about. A beautiful young woman clad in an exquisite sari climbs between two handsome men into the most modern semi I have yet seen in India.

People stare at us, but no one crowds in around us.

We order chai and samosas, then sit back to do a bit of staring ourselves. Tacked to a post directly across from our table is this establishment's only adornment, a painting in vivid color of Vishnu and his wife, Lakshmi, reclining together in comfortable, almost erotic attire. Vishnu's broad perfect chest is bare to the waist. The picture hangs in striking contrast with the surrounding homeliness, otherwise mitigated only by the natural beauty of the forest beyond.

After we get back on the bike, we come upon another assemblage of pilgrims tramping by along the road. This mostly male entourage is dressed in fairly modern western style city attire, windbreakers, slacks, shirts that button down the front. Besides the red spots in the middle of their foreheads, the one common feature of their attire is that they are all wearing identical yellow baseball caps.

"Why do you suppose pilgrims wear baseball hats?" I ask Dick.

"To shade their eyes from the sun."

"I know. But the style doesn't seem to have much religious symbolism."

"This must be a more practical group."

"Maybe they aren't pilgrims, just volksmarcher or something," I suggest.

"No. They're pilgrims. India doesn't have volksmarches."

"They once had a salt march," I assert.

"That was a long time ago."

"Maybe this is a peace march or a protest of some sort."

"Why would they wear baseball caps for a protest march?" Dick says.

"To shade their eyes from the sun."

"No. This is a pilgrimage. If it were a protest, they would be carrying signs."

Off and on throughout the afternoon, we see more people walking along the road wearing the same identical type of baseball caps. By mid-afternoon, the road becomes windy and begins to descend from the Deccan plateau down toward the coastal lowlands. The terrain levels out again, and woodlands give way to a desolate yellow plane stretching to infinity. Far out in the open desert, we still come upon an occasional band of pilgrims in baseball caps. Many smile and wave as we skim past them.

As the sun sinks lower in the sky, we spot a building out in the middle of nowhere with a sign saying, "Saihapur Hotel." Three large buses are parked in front. A group of ball-capped pilgrims chats nearby.

"I hope this is really a hotel," says Dick. By now, we have figured out that the English word "hotel" in India is used to designate a broad category of establishments in the hospitality industry, most often a restaurant.

The front side of the building is open to the air, so we lean the bike against a lamp post and walk in together. The building apparently consists of one large room with lots of tables but no adjoining rooms. One of the pilgrims, a gentleman in his forties, stands in front near the pay counter holding his yellow cap and waving it about as he talks with a man behind the counter. He speaks in an authoritative tone as though he must be an organizer of the pilgrimage. "Ah," he says. "Here are the people with the wonderful bicycle. Our friends have seen you on the road." News travels fast in India, even among walkers. But now I notice a small radio protruding from the man's breast pocket. These pilgrims with baseball caps are modern in other ways as well.

"What country are you from?" he asks.

"America."

"America! That is a wonderful bicycle. By the year 2030, we may have such a bicycle in India! I will have one then." He still holds his cap, waving it around by the bill as he speaks.

"I have seen many caps like yours on the road today," I say. "Why do you wear baseball caps on a pilgrimage?"

"This is good to shield our eyes from the sun," he says.

"Surely. But why yellow and why are there so many exactly alike?

"Oh, yes. You see, our group is very large, and there are many pilgrims on the road. This helps the driver to recognize us when he brings the car with food and water."

"How far have you walked on your pilgrimage?" asks Dick.

"We come from Shirdi, one hundred and fifty kilometers. These buses will take us to the next town where we will spend the night."

"That was a long walk," I say."

"We have been gone four days."

"You must be very tired," I say.

The man grimaces and and gestures with the hat toward his feet. "Yes. My feet have many sores."

Our eyes follow his gesture down to his feet. He isn't barefoot like the Jain monks, but he isn't equipped with Rockports or Nikes either. Instead he wears a pair of loafers with little support and no laces. "Those shoes don't look very comfortable," I observe.

The man frowns. "Very painful," he says. He slides his foot out of the shoe. It is covered with a white sock whose ankles have turned yellow from the dust. The heel is swollen with bulges of bandages underneath.

He gently stuffs the foot back in the shoe and looks at me. "But you too must be tired. How far you come on your bicycle?"

"From Agra."

"From Agra! That's a very long way."

"We are biking for a cause," says Dick. He shows the pilgrim our newspaper articles.

The man looks at the articles. "Yes, someone saw your banner on the road. You bike for peace. You too are pilgrims. Did you visit the shrine at Shirdi?"

"We planned to go there but took a wrong turn."

"Shame. Such a beautiful shrine to Sai Baba is there."

"Where do you pilgrims sleep at night?" I ask, hoping to steer the conversation around to the business at hand. I can see the sun peering over a window sill at the back of the restaurant.

The pilgrim leans back with his palms spread out, facing the sky. "We sleep in the open," he says.

This brings Dick back to business. He turns to the man behind the counter. "Is there lodging here, someplace to spend the night?"

The man smiles, nods and points up the road. "Yes. Lodging. Thirty kilometers."

"Thirty kilometers is too far. We are traveling by bicycle. It will be dark soon," says Dick.

Imitating the pilgrim's gesture, I look toward the sky, palms facing upward. "Perhaps we can sleep in the open," I say.

The pilgrim raises his brow and curls his lip as though he has an idea. "Are you prepared to sleep in the open?"

"Sure," I say. "So long as there are no crowds."

"Crowds?"

"No people crowding around us."

"But there are dangerous insects," says the man.

"We have mosquito netting," says Dick.

"Would the cold be a problem?"

"We have warm clothing," I assure him. Actually, I have only a sweater and a wind breaker, but the temperature is warmer here at this moment than it generally ever gets in Seattle.

The pilgrim turns to the man behind the counter and begins speaking to him persuasively in the local dialect. The man shrugs, shakes his head, seems to object but finally nods reluctant agreement. My guess is that this man behind the counter is not really the person in authority and doesn't have the final say. Yet he somehow feels obligated to cooperate with the pilgrim who is perhaps of higher status, maybe a higher caste or possibly a religious leader.

The pilgrim turns back to us. "Come," he says gesturing for us to follow. He leads us past a white marble shrine to Sai Baba and around to the far side of the restaurant, revealing a scene I can hardly believe. Surely this must be a mirage or oasis in the desert! Tucked between the restaurant and the vast brown plain is a small verdant garden surrounded by a waist high stone wall. Its floor is a soft green lawn with a border of flowering shrubs and young fruit trees. "You can sleep here," says the gentleman, waving his hat at the green lawn.

"Thank you very much," I say. It is the most inviting bedroom I have yet seen in India.

* * * *

I sit on the garden wall watching the sun drop below the brown and empty horizon. Because nothing is perfect, least of all in the real India, there is a generous supply of the usual trash, plastic bags, and pop cans spread over the brown earth beyond the wall. In the midst of the litter half-sits, half-lies, a collapsed, rusted shed of corrugated tin with a few scrawny long horned cows milling about. But trash doesn't bother me now that I am beginning to catch a glimpse of truth from that ultimate state of holiness known as *humbler than dust*. I have a bit of clean green lawn on which to lay my weary head. What more can I ask?

I work on my diary while Dick ties our mosquito netting to a little peach tree to make a tent. I am breathing fairly well now. Maybe the antibiotics are winning. Meanwhile I read a sad, amusing entry in my diary from a few nights before in the town of Ojhar:

> *I'm feeling pretty nauseated now from the antihistamines. I could not force myself to eat this evening. We have come to an impoverished little place called Ojhar. I refer to Ojhar as a place because I almost hesitate to call it a town. It is one of those many places in India that was probably never planned. It just happened. I would be surprised if there has ever been a blueprint before putting up a building in Ojhar.*

But after it got dark, the place lit up (electric lights every-
where) and came alive with pedestrians like Broadway in
Seattle. The darkness totally masked the shabbiness. We could
only see lights, not hovels. People walked around having a good
time, doing their business. We found a fairly decent hotel and
someone led us to a nearby restaurant. Luckily I had Dick's
arm to hang onto or I might not have made it that far. How-
ever, upon setting foot into the restaurant, I was overcome by
the air, heavy with smoking grease, and my body gave way in-
stantly to its annoying gag reflex. So here I am at the door of
this restaurant—this one actually did have a door—gagging
violently as though I was about to lose my lunch. (Fortunately I
had been unable to eat lunch or I surely would have.)

I backed out of the restaurant and sat down on the stoop—
this restaurant actually did have a stoop. Meanwhile, poor Dick
was inside apologizing to the proprietor that his wife was sick
and needed to be outside in the fresh air. "Tomorrow take her
to medical clinic. Shot will fix her up," the man said.

Dick had a good time making friends with the local
Ojharians while I sat outside staring at the sewer. Someone
brought me a delicious bowl of tomato soup which I managed
to get down. However, I could not eat the bread croutons, so I
dropped them in the dirt just short of the sewer. A languid,
mangy dog loped by and ate them, then looked up at me mourn-
fully begging for more. The dog was of the plain brown variety,
the common denominator of stray dogness that roams the streets
of India. If anyone ever feels an impulse to pet one of these god
forsaken creatures, I'm sure it passes quickly. But perhaps from
the Gandhian perspective, these dogs are reincarnated truth
seekers. If anything is humbler than dust, it's them.

In contrast with that dismal evening, I am in heaven now. I feel
much better and have a good appetite for the delicious looking
Saihapur menu. I look forward to green salad and rice with lentils
for dinner and to enjoying the loveliest bedroom in India.

After Dick finishes constructing our mosquito-netting tent, we
make our bed inside by spreading out our silk sleeping bag liner and

covering that with the same two small blankets on which Dick lays out the parts when assembling the bike. That will be sufficient for this warm night.

On our way back into the restaurant, we visit the shrine to Sai Baba of Shirdi which is located along the sidewalk. About the size and shape of a typical Indian snack and beverage stall, its walls are covered with glimmering white marble tiles. Draped in a red robe and hung with garlands, the statue of Sai Baba sits on an altar of white marble surrounded by shiny copper and bronze incense burners. His face and thick lips are painted white, the heavy eye brows, black. Flanking either side of the statue are two photographs of the same avatar.

The photos echo the statue's facial features almost as if they have been placed there to verify its authenticity. They are clearly all the same face. Yet I would not have picked him out of a lineup of strangers as the one most likely to embody spiritual perfection and the epitome of compassion. If it were not for the robes and garlands, I would judge this to be the face of a logger or coal miner, a simple man who has been through enough hardship to remain calm in the face of adversity. His is the face of someone with average intelligence at best. But maybe that's the point. Sai Baba is said to have lived a simple life sitting under the margosa tree, walking in the woods, being fed by others, giving away everything to the poor, thinking only of today. Because he was so much like that, people decided he was the incarnation of God. When they first began to revere him as such, he objected but learned, in time, to tolerate the attention.

Sai Baba of Shirdi, who died in 1918, is not to be mistaken for Satya Sai Baba of Puttaparthi, born in 1926. At 16 years of age, Satya Sai Baba claimed to be the reincarnation of the Shirdi avatar and therefore the incarnation of God. Given to sleight of hand and materializing objects out of thin air, Satya commands a large following. However his authenticity has been called into question. Some former devotees have accused him of sexual exploitation.

When I think of Satya Sai Baba, I am reminded of Mr. Menom's warning, "Some of them are fakes." But, whether or not the allegations are true, and whether or not Satya Sai Baba is for real, my point here is that Satya is not the gentleman to whom the baseball capped pilgrims and this restaurant owner with his simple country shrine are devoted. Shirdi Sai Baba is their man, or rather I should say, their god.

From inside the restaurant, a monotonous melodic chant to Shirdi Sai Baba has been playing over and over since we arrived. At sunset, several men come out and perform a ritual in the shrine, lighting incense and placing blossoms in a bowl before the statue. Then they sing a responsive chant as darkness falls. I would like to join them, but I have no authentic red spot on my forehead, and I haven't been invited.

After dinner, Dick and I crawl joyously into our little mosquito netting tent. It is about the same size as the tent we use for back packing the mountains of Washington State. This feels like a comfortable ritual, familiar as flossing our teeth. But the special feature of this tent is its transparency. The tent and sleeping gear we use back home seals us off into a tiny cocoon to keep out the cold. By contrast, this cobweb of mosquito netting leaves us open to the beauty of what seems a warm summer night even though it is the middle of January. We look up through the skinny branches of peach tree saplings coated with feather-like leaves as though they were wings ready to take us aloft into a black sky filled with stars. We recognize Cassiopeia and the big dipper and wonder about thousands of other constellations we cannot name. Rolling over on my side to fall asleep, I can see the soft yellow glow of lamps along the walkway leading to the shrine.

* * * *

Rustling movements and the jingling of keys awaken me in the night. Through my half closed eyes, I can still see the row of lamps, but one of them appears to come alive and fly swiftly toward me. Now it is only a few feet away shining directly in my face and I realize it is not one of the lamps but rather a large flash light.

"*Kubai! Kubai aloo!*" commands a powerful male voice. At least *Kubai aloo* is the sound that I think I have heard. Although I have long since given up on Indian languages, I am fairly sure of the man's meaning. "What the hell are you doing here?" It's either that or he's telling me I'm under arrest.

"*Kubai! Kubai aloo!*" He shouts again louder this time.

"English," I say. "I'm sorry. I only speak English," The words sputter from my mouth, weak and helpless.

The flashlight beam moves out of my face and down across our tent. Then it flies over to illuminate our luggage that leans against a tree. Next it travels along the shiny blue frame of our bike.

I can see the man, although not clearly. He wears the olive green, precisely pressed clothing of so many police officers I have seen in India. Hopefully he will go away and not try to arrest us. Admittedly, there would be a bed in his jail, but I much prefer sleeping out here in the beautiful Saihapur Hotel garden.

While the policeman turns and moves away with his flashlight complaining to himself, I imagine his self-talk during the entire interaction.

What the nerve! Homeless beggars taking unwelcome advantage . . . sleeping in the Saihpur Hotel garden I am charged to protect from them . . . strange, a white head above the covers . . . elderly person . . . old woman's voice . . . English? . . . an English woman? . . . expensive piece of mosquito netting . . . quite new . . . strange . . . other expensive luggage . . . weird looking machine . . . what? . . . a shiny bicycle! what? . . . one cycle . . . two seats, two pairs of pedals . . . now I've seen everything. Someone should have told me they were given permission to sleep here. The nerve of them not telling me! How can I do my job if no one keeps me informed?

And so he grumbles away, cursing to himself.

It is fully daylight when I wake up again. Dick is awake too, so after only a bit of cuddling, we get up and start packing our things. While we munch our boiled eggs and bananas, the men come out from the restaurant and perform their early morning ritual at the shrine. We can hear them chanting, singing, and praying as we quietly push the bike across the garden and out into the road.

CHAPTER 19

Schweda of Kurla,
A Twenty-First Century Woman

Adorning the right-of-way into Bombay is an oil pipeline several feet in diameter. We ride into town on what appears to be a freeway. However, most of the fast moving traffic sticks to the center lanes leaving the periphery to slow pokes like us. This gives us a long, painful view of what car drivers skim by unaware. A murky open sewer runs along between the highway and a row of makeshift, *put up whatever you can find* sort of dwellings. But life goes on here as much as anywhere else. Bikes, rickshaws, motorcycles, now and then even a salvaged automobile or two, are parked between the dwellings. Children stir about with their hands in the sewer water and play in garbage a foot deep. An old woman churns the rank, murky liquid with a broom stick, possibly looking for something she dropped in it by mistake.

The map shows Kurla, the neighborhood where our Servas host Sushama Bajpai lives, to be on the opposite side of the freeway. To get over there we have to detach the bike from the trailer, haul it down a steep flight of stairs, cross under via a tunnel, and drag everything back up. Dick takes the bike and I the trailer. Groups of passers-by team up to help. They yell, push, yank, and shove in uncoordinated effort whenever a trailer wheel gets caught on a broken step or pothole.

When we get to the Kurla railway station, we are greeted by a most unruly mob. Sushama had suggested we just ask someone at the train station for directions to her address. After all, she had never seen us before, let alone our two-seater bike. I suppose she couldn't picture us as a street side-show. So it is a pretty typical day, one to make us grateful we need not live through many more like it. At long last, we are in Bombay.

When we finally arrive at Sushama's fifth floor apartment, her nineteen-year-old daughter, Schweda, greets us at the door in the poised and friendly manner of someone very much at home in the world. She does not have the Bollywood glamour of the Tiwari daughters, but there is a wholesome beauty about her. Her jaw is square, and her body has the planted look of an Earth Mother. Explaining in relaxed, perfect English that her mother is still at work, Schweda directs us to lock our bike to a tree inside the courtyard. Then she recruits a young man from the neighborhood to help us upstairs with the luggage.

As we settle in and relax with Schweda over tea and cookies, I cannot say that I feel the slightest trace of sadness to be so near the end of our journey. Maybe there'll be a twinge of nostalgia on some future, dark Seattle winter evening after the hardships and hassles of this trip have sifted out of memory. As for now, I feel nothing but sublime relief.

Although Sushama had described her home as "a large flat," the tidy and tastefully simple living room barely holds its single bed, an attractive wall storage unit, and two plastic chairs. A wall poster with colorful topsy-turvy letters proclaims, "Don't tidy up my mess. You'll foul up the system." The words seem poignantly humorous in this orderly room containing so few objects. It would be more appropriate in a typical American home stuffed to the gills with extraneous consumer products from Wal-Mart. Or better yet, it belongs in Dick's study where every inch of shelving and floor is piled high with books and papers.

"You will have dinner tonight at my grandmother's house," Schweda says. "She lives in the building just around the corner. But between now and then my mother told me to find out if you have errands to accomplish in preparation for the World Social Forum. I can take you where you need to go."

"I have to find an Internet café," says Dick. He seldom stays offline for more than a few hours at a time. By stopping at every possible Internet café along our route from Agra he has juggled enough email to schedule and coordinate several workshops and panels on global democracy at the Forum. He has also arranged with an organization called the "Alliance for a Responsible, Plural, and United World" to reserve our lodging. He says the Alliance has promised to pay for us to stay a few days at a place called the Inter-continental Hotel.

"I need to buy a dress," I say.

Dick gives me a startled look. "A dress?" He knows I'm not fond of dresses.

"Yes, I'd like one of those Indian dresses with pants underneath." I can't make speeches and conduct workshops in my tan nylon pants, all permanently stained and threadbare from the road.

"A Punjabi dress," says Schweda. " I know where to get a nice one."

"Also, I think I should see a doctor again. Even though I took the full round of antibiotics, I still have a sinus infection that just won't go away."

"We have a wonderful family doctor," says Schweda. I would want you to meet him anyway. He is like a father to me."

* * * *

I walk beside Schweda through the streets of Kurla, trying to view the neighborhood from her viewpoint as the normal stressless place she has lived in all her life. In many ways, modern city planners would view this as a fine, sustainable urban environment. Apartment buildings, four or five stories high, are grouped attractively around intervening open space in easy walking distance from a vibrant market district with a railway station that connects this to other neighborhoods and towns. On the corner, Schweda hails an auto rickshaw that will dispatch us quickly to accomplish our errands. There is no need for anyone to have a gas-guzzling automobile. In fact there are virtually no single occu-pancy cars in sight.

Maybe Schweda doesn't even notice the soot blackened stucco walls, the litter, the lack of playgrounds, shrubs, or grass. As a child, she probably played calmly, as today's Indian children do, amongst the debris. To her, television and movie scenes sans garbage are imaginary places like Camelot.

As for the auto rickshaw ride, Schweda sits calmly with her hands folded in her lap. She doesn't wonder why there is nothing to hold onto, let alone no seat belts, as we round the corner and charge into a frantic destruction derby of rickshaws, motorcycles, and buses. Mountains of bricks, sand, and dirt piled in front of stores, people walking among the busy traffic, the shrieking and honking of horns are all normal and necessary trappings of commerce in the vibrant community where she has lived all her life.

After a good fifteen or twenty minute ride, we stop in front of the dress shop. Schweda calmly pays the driver without any haggling over the cost. She doesn't even have to ask the cost for she knows standard charge for this quarter-hour carnival ride. Schweda has been doing errands this way all her life. Following her example I try to enjoy myself. I tell her, "Our Seattle neighborhood is so boring compared with Kurla."

Without Schweda's help I would never have found the dress shop. Its signs are beautifully painted in Hindi. From the outside, it looks like any other stall. Except that there is a glass front over this stall with a door to open and walk in. There are no racks of dresses for customers to paw through as in a U.S. dress shop. Instead, the walls are lined with shelves stacked full of flat cellophane wrapped rectangles of every imaginable color. After Schweda explains that I am looking for a Punjabi dress, the proprietor asks what color.

I shrug. "Blue . . . maybe green . . . perhaps purple."

The proprietor searches his shelves and pulls out three rectangles, one of each color I had mentioned, and sets them on the counter. The colors seem to leap out of their cellophane containers along with shiny gold trim and embroidered floral designs in many enhancing colors. I look at them lying there at chest level, all neatly folded. They are certainly beautiful, like works of art in a gallery. I am reluctant to disturb them, but I am unwilling to buy a dress

without trying it on first. "Is it possible to try this on?" I ask, pointing to a resplendent blue one. "Yes," of course," says Schweda. There
is a dressing room in the back."

"Please try them all," says the man.

I'm pretty sure that the blue is one is best for me, but I take
them all back with me just in case the blue one doesn't fit.

Back in the dressing room, I am astounded to witness the spilling of so much fabric from such a tight little package. Besides the
embroidered dress with its stiff gold trim, there is a pair of pants
with an adjustable waistline ample enough to accommodate preg-
nancy, overeating, growing older, or any other growth challenge.
Fitting will not be a problem. There is also a matching blue dupatta
or shawl trimmed in the same shiny gold and large enough for a
bedspread. At the quoted cost of 750 rupees ($15.00), this is an
incredible bargain.

* * * *

After another exciting fifteen-minute rickshaw ride, we arrive at
the doctor's waiting room situated in the back courtyard of an apartment complex. People sit on plastic chairs and wooden benches
along the wall. A receptionist is perched on a stool at the counter up
front. She tells us the doctor has been called away on an emergency
and may not be back for more than an hour.

I glance at Schweda for any sign of irritation. She must have
other things to do besides take care of me. After all, she is a full-time
university student majoring in commerce and also works part-time
as a product demonstrator at a convention center. But Schweda settles
back comfortably in her chair. "You will have time to tell me all
about your travels while we wait," she says. "What do you think is
the most remarkable thing about India?"

It's an open-ended question, so I wait to see what surfaces from
the flood of experiences over the past couple of months. The word
"garbage" emerges first but I shove it back under. "Spirituality," I
say. "I have never imagined a place as spiritual as India." Then it
occurs to me that, since Schweda has never been out of India, the
spirituality is every bit as much a part of the landscape to her as
garbage and stray animals. It is probably hard for her to imagine a
place as irreligious as a typical U.S. shopping mall. Because her

mother belongs to Servas, I know the family must be open-minded, but I wonder how they feel about religion. "Is your family religious?" I ask.

"Oh, yes. We are very religious."

"How often do you visit the temple?"

"Three times a week, Tuesdays, Thursdays, and Saturdays."

"What do you do there?"

"Do?"

"Yes, like in our church, we sing and listen to a sermon. What do you do in your temple?"

She laughs and shakes her head. "We don't sing or listen to a sermon. We just stay a few minutes to pray. We bow and show respect to the god. We offer the god gifts of flower petals and oil lamps. I always give a sweet, some fruit to the god and then to myself. This is symbolic. It means that you respect the power of god and admit that you need his help."

So now, it's time for my naive question again, the one Gaurau didn't have time to fully answer before the light came on in his garden. The question has been burning in my mind ever since. "What is a god?" I ask.

Schweda smiles in the same embarrassed way Gaurau had. "God is the spirit that made the universe."

Her answer is, almost word for word, the same as Gaurau's. Perhaps now, with at least an hour to wait for the doctor, no one will interrupt the next part of the question. "Then why are there so many gods? Hinduism is a very confusing religion," I say. Could the *spirit that sustains the universe* be a plurality?

Schweda laughs. "Yes. Hinduism is very confusing," she says. "There are many spiritual powers in the universe. There are many people in India. The reason there are so many gods is because each person has a different idea of god. There needs to be some way for everyone to relate to god in their own way. That's why even Buddha and Jesus are part of the Hindu pantheon. We don't exclude anyone's idea of god."

"Wow! That's religious tolerance!" I say. "That's the same religion I believe in. Back home we call ourselves Unitarians. All these years I thought I was a Unitarian, but now I know that I am really a

Hindu at heart." I reach in my pocket, pull out a tube of pink lip-gloss and paint a little spot in the middle of my forehead. "There, I'm a Hindu."

Schweda laughs again, but this time in a more embarrassed way. I worry that my gesture might be perceived as flippant or disre-spectful, so I reach for my handkerchief and try to wipe away the spot. But Schweda continues in complete empathy with my feel-ings. "At heart we are all the same religion. As Gandhi says, 'We are all part of the same human family.'"

"Have you always been religious?"

"Oh, no. There was a time when I would refuse to go to the temple. I was very depressed then about my life."

Our conversation is interrupted by the receptionist announcing that the doctor has arrived, but Schweda continues. "It was my doc-tor who helped most. He told me I have only one life to live. He told me that I must use my talents and realize my potential. He said if bad feelings interfere with what I am trying to do, I must change them because they will destroy my health. He suggested that I pray every day to Ganesh for guidance. Hindus pray to Ganesh ask-ing him to remove obstacles in their paths. Ganesh represents the universal power to remove obstacles that block our way in life. When I pray to Ganesh and place flowers at his shrine, I submit my obstacles up to the universe, trusting in the wisdom of god's creation."

I think about this simple gesture of faith, offering her obstacles up to the universe. It sounds like the Alcoholics Anonymous idea of ad-mitting that there are things in life you can't control, so you surrender them to a *higher power*. Maybe that is the central function of any reli-gious faith. "You have a very good doctor. He knows there's more to healing than pills and shots. Most American family doctors stick to pharmaceuticals. If you're depressed, they might refer you to a psychia-trist, but they tend to stay away from spiritual guidance. Yet faith is probably the most crucial component of healing."

A woman enters wearing a plain, rumpled sari. She carries in her arms a little boy about two years of age. The child cries as if in severe pain. He writhes in his mother's arms as she sits down on a bench across from us.

"The baby is very sick," Schweda observes sadly.

The mother cradles the toddler against her chest and wraps her sari around him. He stops crying and starts to nurse.

"Indian people seem to be good parents," I say. "Will you marry and have children one day?" I think about the Tiwari daughters and their eight-thousand-dollar dowries. I know Sushama works in a bank. Maybe she cannot afford this for Schweda.

"Perhaps I will marry, perhaps not. Either way, I plan to earn my own way," says Schweda.

"I've heard it's very expensive for the family when a woman gets married in India."

"Yes, it can cost many thousands of rupees. I have told my parents they must not pay that. I will make my own life. I am responsible for my own happiness. Some day I may find a love match, but I am not looking for that."

I listen in awe of Schweda's views on life and marriage. Either she is a woman of great courage or society's values are far more modern here in Bombay than in the countryside.

The receptionist interrupts us again with an announcement in Hindi. "It's now your turn to go in and see the doctor," says Schweda.

I am disappointed that our wait is over. But I am excited to meet Schweda's father figure, her special healer. At the receptionist's invitation, Schweda comes in with me.

The consultation room is even smaller and plainer than the waiting room. There is a desk, but the doctor isn't sitting behind it. He steps forward to greet Schweda lovingly as though she were indeed his daughter. He has a plump, fatherly face with kindly intelligent eyes. The three of us stand facing one another while the doctor inquires about the health of everyone in Sushama's family. Then he invites me to lie down on a chest-high cot while he stands beside me looking through instruments into my nostrils. "Your nasal passages are red and swollen," he says. "How long have you had these symptoms?"

I explain the history of my sinus problems, how it started several weeks ago in Chennai . . . or were those the first symptoms in Sawai Modhopur? . . . how the symptoms have grown better and worse from time to time but have never gone away. I show him my empty punch card of antibiotics.

The doctor shakes his head sympathetically. "The air in India is hard to breathe," he says. "Your nose is not accustomed to it. When you get home to familiar air, your nose will be itself again."

"But in the meantime I have to make speeches, conduct workshops and meetings at the World Social Forum."

The doctor nods sympathetically. "I will write you a prescription for a stronger antibiotic. You will make good speeches. Mrs. Bajpai has told me you will speak about democracy is it?"

"Yes, global democracy. We want to create a world parliament elected by the people."

The doctor rubs some invisible whiskers on his chin. Then he says, "Democracy is a grand ideal, but hard to put into practice."

"We believe that democracy at the international level would strengthen democracy at the national and local levels."

"In India only poor, uneducated people vote. Educated people take a holiday on election day. That's why we don't have enlightened leadership. That's why, for instance, we cannot clean up the slums."

"It is the opposite in America," I say. "Poor people don't vote. That's why we have leadership that favors the rich. But why would poor people vote against cleaning up the slums?"

"Well, for one reason, to clean up the slums, we would need laws to prevent them from building more slums. That would greatly inconvenience a lot of folks during the monsoon season when they need to put up a bit of shelter from the rain."

"For democracy to work, you need a truly educated electorate. Even so, I'm not ready to give up. Democracy would be such a good deal if we could ever make it happen," I say.

The doctor smiles and nods like an elder approving the idealism of youth.

Schweda says, "I'm so glad you are not giving up on democracy. The world would be a desperate place if there were no hope for it."

The doctor agrees in a tone tempered by skepticism. "Yes, and your global parliament idea would be good for India. After all, we have a large portion of the world's population."

As the doctor writes out the prescription, I reach in my pack for my wallet and ask him what the cost will be. The doctor waves his palm downward. "No charge. You are here to help my country."

I am astounded to receive a free consultation from a medical doctor. In America this would never happen. The magnanimity of India never ceases to amaze me.

* * * *

It is dark by the time we leave the doctor's office so the auto rickshaw ride is even scarier. I am reminded of our first automobile ride in Agra. Darting about in a torrent of moving lights, it had felt like a scene from *Star Wars*. But then we were protectively armored inside an automobile with solid windows and doors.

Thus exposed to battle, Schweda sits in poised serenity. This, after all, is the way she has gone to school just before dawn every morning of her life. What's new? Following her example, I pretend as though we are just doing this for fun.

We have to stop for a long wait at a pharmacy stall to get my prescription filled, so it is well into the dinner hour when we arrive at Schweda's grandmother's apartment. The living room is full of people, mostly her beautiful Indian family. Besides Schweda's grandfather, her mother, Sushama, is there as well as her aunt and uncle who live upstairs. Dick is there and so is Toto, Sushama's other Servas guest, a tall skinny senior citizen from Italy. The grandmother goes and comes happily back and forth from the kitchen while everyone else participates in lively discussion. They have long since crossed the name/number of children/profession threshold of conversation and have launched into the inevitable subject of politics. Dick is enjoying himself and barely allows the conversation to lapse long enough to acknowledge our arrival and make introductions.

The grandfather asks Dick what he thinks of Vajpayee, the Indian Prime Minister. "It's hard for us to judge him. We hear so little about Indian politics in the U.S.," says Dick. "But Vajpayee at least is trying to make peace with Pakistan. We are grateful for that."

Toto says, "Yes, Vajpayee tries to make peace while your government makes war."

"Perhaps our leaders should learn from Vajpayee," says Dick.

"Will you get a new president at the next election?" Sushama asks.

"I think there is a good chance," says Dick.

"Will it be Hillary Clinton?" asks Schweda.

Dick laughs and shakes his head. We have been asked this question often in India.

I say, "Perhaps one day she will run, but not this year. She has only been a Senator for less than one term. She needs more seniority to be in the running."

Schweda's uncle says, "Then there will be no change. Mrs. Clinton alone has the name familiarity to beat the incumbent."

"Not necessarily so," says Dick. "Several others are running. Howard Dean is getting a lot of press attention right now."

This draws confused silence for a moment while Schweda's grandmother brings in a plate of chapatis.

Schweda says, "Who is Howard Dean?"

"The governor of Vermont," says Dick.

More silence while people start nibbling chapatis, their bewilderment still hanging in the air. Apparently even Vermont has little name familiarity in India, let alone its governor.

Schweda says, "This makes little sense to us in India. For instance, if someone is going to defeat Vajpayee, it will have to be Sonia Gandhi. Everyone has heard the name, Gandhi. Why would some unknown nobody become your president?"

"I don't know," I say. "Maybe it's because we don't have a name like Gandhi to fall back on."

CHAPTER 20

Giants with Dirty Toes

We start out this morning in search of the Intercontinental Hotel with nothing more than Schweda's waving us in the general direction. "It's about ten kilometers over that way near the airport." She bows, prayer hands forward. "Namaste," she says. "I will pray to Ganesh for your success at the forum. He will remove all obstacles in your path." I want very much to give her a hug.

There was a time, not so very long ago, when Dick would not have tried to find the corner drugstore without a map. Maybe that Dick died with the one who preferred picnic lunches way out in the countryside to being mobbed at village food stands. This new road-hardened Dick will go anywhere, do anything. We stop at every corner to flag down one of the auto rickshaws or motorcycles swarming round us and yell, "Airport? Intercontinental Hotel?"

The most frequent response is a blank stare followed by a cannon fire of Hindi. If we are lucky, the driver points or waves in a perceivable direction while delivering the volley of Hindi. This goes on for several hours before Dick announces that we have traveled in a circle halfway around the airport without ever spotting either the Hyatt or the Intercontinental, reportedly two of the tallest buildings in Bombay. I take this ordeal very much in stride, reassuring myself that this might well be our last bike ride in India.

Oh, Joy! Now we are passing the Hyatt! Where there is a Hyatt, there must be an airport. The Intercontinental Hotel cannot be far away. The Hyatt is a giant of modern corporate opulence. His feet are smeared in the barren, humble dust of ramshackle huts, cows drinking from puddles of brackish water, people milling about, children in rags playing cricket with splintered wooden sticks. Even after two months in India, it is still hard to believe my eyes. To think that from that tower of windows the wealthiest elite gaze down with bare eyeballs upon this display of inequality!

Last night at dinner, Sushama's Italian guest, Toto, who is a world traveler, had mentioned that other countries like China hide their poor. India does not. "Urban renewal projects," he said, "Do not improve the lives of poor people. They just hide the poor so the better off don't have to look at them."

I wonder why India doesn't hide its poor. Perhaps there are too many or maybe, as Schweda's doctor suggested, they vote against being hid.

Just past the Hyatt, we turn left into a divided street with a planting strip of flowers in the middle. Towering over our heads is another neoteric monstrosity with a pretentious label sprawled across its shoulders, *Intercontinental the Grand Hotel.* A mandate blips across my conscience that I cannot stay in such a place. But that thought is barely formed before it evaporates. By latest estimates, the World Social Forum expects to enroll upwards of a hundred thousand people. Every imaginable sleeping room in the entire city is already booked. It isn't like we have another choice. Beside, a group of strangers calling themselves "Alliance for a Responsible, Plural, and United World," has reserved us a room at this hotel.

The taxi drivers in front of the Intercontinental Hotel stare in disbelief as a weird, blue, double-seated, pedal-powered contraption pulls into the driveway. It pulls behind it a trailer draped with a banner whose logo is obscured by layers of dust. An elderly white couple disembarks. They wear red and white helmets smeared with axle grease. Their stained slacks and T-shirts look as though they have never been pressed and might disintegrate at any moment.

The gentleman approaches the doorman and announces with casual abandon, "We want to check into the hotel. We have a reservation for two."

I watch the doorman's sober face dissolve into a road map of smile lines. His black mustache twitches with mirth. Wearing a period costume, complete with a two-foot red turban, gold braid and a column of gold buttons down the front of his tunic, the doorman is the biggest Indian I have ever seen. "Yes, please come in." He opens the big glass door and bows gallantly, his curly black mustache still bobbing with amusement.

As usual, Dick goes in to register while I wait in front holding up the bike. In front of much shabbier small town hotels, I have drawn crowds doing this. Once a dog had singled me out and had begun to bark ferociously at my heels. The street had been full of traffic, but I looked so strange that even the dog knew I did not belong. This time, there are no crowds or dogs, just a few taxi drivers and a very impressive doorman.

The doorman insists, "Please go in, Madame."

"The bike has no kickstand," I explain. "It will fall over."

The doorman says, "I will hold it up for you until your husband comes back."

Inside the lobby, I gawk like a country bumpkin on his first visit to the city. Or like a gnome who has wandered into the world of the big folk, I blink at the high atrium encircled by several stories of balconies with hundreds of doors overlooking gigantic works of art.

At one end of the room are huge oil paintings of famous buildings in downtown Bombay. These works must be rendered from photographs taken by cameras angled upward away from the poverty in the streets. In fact, the tops of the lampposts are at the bottoms of the pictures. The *real* India, the one at street level, is intentionally omitted. On the opposite wall is a seven story mosaic featuring birds, trees, clouds, ocean waves, beauties of the natural world again focused upward and outward beyond the level of base human existence. Awe struck by this ethereal artistry, it crosses my mind that maybe the way folks remain sane in India is by walking around gazing upward. In fact, a lot of them are off in yogic trances looking into divine nirvana.

The best way to get away from street grime, however, would be to check into this hotel, if you happen to be part of that tiniest percentage of Indians who could afford to. I take a deep, clean breath. The finest air-filtering system money can buy has created a pristine microclimate in here for soft golden carpets and dustless marble tables topped with big bouquets of tropical flowers.

"Wow!" I breathe aloud. "This is *not* the real India!" Overhearing me, the doorman's grin erupts into a full-bellied laugh.

The hotel desk clerks are glamorous young women in chic designer saris and carefully applied makeup complete with eye-liner and lipstick to match their pious forehead spots. One hands me a key and invites me to go on up to the room while Dick takes the bicycle down to the parking garage.

"Thank you," I say. But my attention is drawn to a big copper bowl of oranges sitting on the counter. I am very hungry from our harrowing ride across Bombay. "May I have an orange?" I ask.

"Of course, Madame. You are our guest." Even though she doesn't say the words, they echo in my mind from many humbler scenes, "Guest is god."

I take the orange, an offering from and to the gods, along with the key and head for the elevator. Encased in a bubble of glass, the elevator commands a view of the atrium artworks as it rises toward the magnificent canopy of glass skylight. It feels like a hot air balloon ride.

At the sight of our room, two months of road hardening drops away. Body and soul give way to their long-resisted temptation to crumple into a heap of exhaustion. There is no humility here nor one grain of messy old truth. Every last dust-mite has been filtered out of the air. The bedding is soft, white, and fluffy, the furnishing tasteful and comforting. The temperature is almost imperceptible, neither warm nor cold.

One entire wall consists of a draped glass window and doorway opening onto a balcony behind the building. When I pull the cord to open the drapes, sunlight spills onto the floor and over the bed. But that's when I discover that this giant also has dirty toes. Nestled at the back of this lavish development and scattered over the surrounding landscape, is a hovel of dwellings much like those at the foot of the Hyatt across the way, in fact, like much of Bombay. This scene is also complete with its own herds of cows, puddles of brackish water, and ragged children playing cricket.

Next, I open the door to the bathroom. Even before turning on the light, I can see what must be an apparition in the darkness, reflecting particles of light from somewhere beyond like a white marble shrine in the caves of Ellora. Made of sparkling porcelain, clean as a sterilized test tube, but large enough to stretch out the full length of one's body, is the most beautiful bathtub I have ever seen.

By the time Dick arrives, I am already afloat in hot water, soothing every aching muscle, melting away the stress in every neuron, breathing steam into every alveoli of my respiratory system. I can feel my body disappearing. There is nothing left but unperturbed spirit.

After I get out of the tub, I put on the white terry cloth bathrobe that the hotel has provided. Then I lie down in the sunshine pouring over the bed and drift off.

I don't know how much later it is when Dick wakes me up. "It's time for the opening ceremonies at the conference grounds," he says.

I ponder that a moment. We have come a long way. It would be a shame to miss the fanfare, the speeches by Arundhati Roy, Noam Chomsky, Joseph Stiglitz, all those heroes of the anti-globalization movement. But I have heard them before. I must sleep and get well. I'm here to do a job, not to be *infotained*, and as Schweda's doctor pointed out, "It's difficult to work when you are sick."

"I'm sick," I say and close my eyes again.

Next time Dick wakes me up, it is still daylight, but the sun is setting. "I've talked with Rob and Germa. They're staying on the floor above us. Andy and Mr. Chavan are also here in Mumbai, and there is another Indian guy named Biplov who wants to join us. We'll have a meeting to plan our organizational strategy."

"Where will we meet?"

"Downstairs in the lobby."

"That's great!" I say, relieved that I will not have to go back out into the real India today. "How did you arrange all this?"

"There's a room full of computers for the forum delegates staying here in the hotel," he says.

"You are truly remarkable."

"Thanks. How's your nose?"

"Better. This place is a hospital."

"It's priced like one, too. Germa says the Alliance will only reimburse us for three days. The forum lasts a whole week."

"Do we have enough rupees left?"

"Barely. We might have to fall back on the credit card."

* * * *

It has taken awhile for us to gather, but finally most of the players Dick had mentioned are seated under the atrium in a circle of sofas and overstuffed chairs. Professor Andy Strauss (Andy), our international law expert, is the only one still missing, but Dick assures us he will soon be here. Appointing myself as secretary, I take the meeting notes in my diary. It's all part of the same story.

Rob Wheeler, a sort of self-appointed coordinator of our movement, informally chairs the meeting. Foot loose and fancy free in his fifties, Rob is an enigmatic character who seems to live pretty much off the generosity of those who admire his dedication to the cause. Although he is a self-proclaimed pauper, Rob uses every dime of *funding,* as he calls it, to get himself to international conferences like this. He must spend hours every day writing long, vague email missives that are always extremely diplomatic but rarely say much. Yet somehow he almost single-handedly keeps our cause alive with virtually no *funding.*

Rob's job now is to finesse a difference of opinion that has already erupted between Germa and the rest of us. After all, it behooves us to get along with Germa. The promised hotel reimbursement from his organization, the *Alliance for a Responsible, Plural, and United World* is the only financial backing for which any of us can hope.

With my hearing aids turned up to their highest volume, I listen intently to Germa. Speaking in his heavy French accent, he forms the English words as precisely and carefully as if he were trying to carve them out of stone. I don't know who is working harder, him or me, as I strain to fill in the hard Anglo American consonants he almost invariably leaves out of every word. "We have to connect with people in all sectors of civil society, get them to realize how a global parliament would help their movements," he says. "As they come on board, there will be a groundswell towards world parliament."

"You want civil society to create the global people's assembly," says Rob. "That would be great if they would do it."

"That was the idea we started out with at the Hague Appeal for Peace in 1999 and then at the World Trade Organization protest in Seattle later that year," I say. "It's pretty hard to get all these varied groups on our wavelength. There are so many of them, all running around doing their own thing, fighting AIDS, protesting against the World Bank, pressing for land reform. They don't have much energy left for what they see as a distant dream."

"Some are even threatened by the idea of global democracy," puts in Dick. "They don't like anything that smacks of *globalization*."

"I don't think you understand," says Germa. "The World Social Forum itself *is* the proper venue for a world parliament. It is all we have of global democracy. Governments listen. We have enrolled 100,000 people in this Forum all speaking out against global economic policies. This is global democracy."

"But it won't have real legitimacy. It won't have the power to make international law until we have elected representatives to an international body," I say.

Germa says, "If the Forum wills it, it will happen."

"That's so true," I say. "I hope we can convince them. But that may take a long time. Maybe there are some other things we can accomplish in the meantime like . . ."

Andy puffs into the lobby pushing a hand trolley filled with the stacks of articles and handouts he has lugged with him all the way from Philadelphia. His face is red, his bald head shining. Dick, Rob, and I jump up and take turns hugging him. Mr. Chavan, Biplov, and Germa observe us Americans from the safe distance of their chairs. Then they stand and shake hands quite formally with Andy.

"This is Dr. Andrew Strauss, international law professor from Weidener University," says Rob.

"Andy's our guru," says Dick.

One of the peak experiences of my life was meeting Andy at the Hague Appeal for Peace in 1999. A small publisher had just come out with *Alien Child,* my novel that visions toward global democracy. The back cover contained a nice endorsement by Princeton International law professor, Richard Falk. I was sitting in my booth trying to promote my book when Andy stopped by and handed me his paper entitled, *Legitimacy and the Power of Popular Sovereignty.* The co-author was Richard Falk.

Legitimacy and the Power of Popular Sovereignty had spelled out pretty much the same concept Germa has been trying to verbalize just now. It said that if global civil society were to start a democratically elected global people's assembly, that body would not have to be sanctioned by any government. It would have the power to sanction governments. That idea had inspired me then. If Germa has just thought of it, he will soon find out how hard it is to capture the attention of the anti-globalization movement and win them to the cause of a world parliament.

After Andy settles in, Rob says, "We were just talking about what our strategy should be. Germa feels we should focus on making the World Social Forum the venue of world parliament, try to bring global civil society on board with us."

"Like Andy suggested in his paper, *Legitimacy and the Power of Popular Sovereignty,*" I point out.

"Yes," says Andy. "Let's keep trying to do that. There will never be a global parliament unless the people really want it."

Mr. Chavan says, "But Andy, Mona tells me that you want to approach as few as twenty governments asking them to sign a treaty starting the parliament."

"Sure," says Andy. "But it will help to have the people on our side."

"It will not only help, it will be necessary," says Germa.

Mr. Chavan says, "Either way, we must be organized. We must stay focused. I'm getting older. I want to see the human family come closer to that goal in my lifetime. There are so few in our movement. But if we follow Gandhi's example, it will only take a few committed people in each country. First we must identify the twenty to thirty countries and find the people."

Germa grimaces and curls his mouth into an upside down U. "I don't think many people here at the forum will agree with your predetermined plan. They will want to be involved in formulating a plan."

Dick and I look at one another helplessly and shrug. We have been struggling this way in starts and restarts for years. Dick has just finished working with an email group from around the world to put together a charter spelling out operating procedures for a coalition. He was hoping this very week in Mumbai to get folks to accept the charter so we could begin to make decisions and accomplish things. "I suppose that means you don't think people will accept the charter Dick wants to present."

Germa shakes his head "I can't really speak for anyone else, but I cannot sign the Alliance on as part of a coalition whose charter we did not help create. I'm pretty sure other groups will feel the same way."

"I'm afraid you may be right, Germa," I say. "But if we have to start over every five or ten years, if we never can agree on a plan and follow it, we will all be dead before anything is accomplished."

Rob says, "This evening we don't have to decide what we're going to accomplish for the next fifty years, even five years. We only have to plan *this* week. We have five three-hour workshops scheduled for the Forum. Dick has a panel organized for the first three hours. Andy has a panel organized for another. All we have to do now is decide what we're going to do during the other nine hours."

I say, "We can have a citizen input session where we ask people how they think we should get organized and the direction to take. We could write all their suggestions down on flip charts. That will take a good three hours. The rest of the time, we can have organizational meetings to form our coalition,"

To my amazement, everyone, even Germa, agrees. There is no dissent. Ganesh must have put it into our heads to stop arguing. After all, our obstacle in this case is our own stubbornness and lack of humility.

Rob says, "Mona, will you bring the flip charts and facilitate the session?"

"Sure. I can facilitate, but I'll need a couple of record keepers to write on the flip charts."

"We can all take turns," says Biplov. "Rob and I can take the first hour." All eyes suddenly turn on Biplov in a unison look of amazement. This is the first time he has spoken.

* * * *

The Goregaon Conference Center *is* the real India. On the first morning of full day conference sessions, we stand ankle deep in the dust of truth just inside the entrance to Building A-7. The plenary was scheduled to start here an hour ago in this huge concrete building. Cobwebs and grease smear the girders supporting its high metal roof. It is the sort of building in which you might expect to view livestock at a country fair. So far, no speakers or forum officials have shown up. Technicians are still hooking up the sound system by means of which they occasionally apologize for an additional delay of indefinite duration.

The morning's program consists of a panel of international law experts including one British journalist, George Monbiot, who favors a world parliament. Hoping the audience might be potential recruits to our cause, Dick and I stayed up last night in our hotel room stuffing Andy's attractive flyers with the schedule of our workshops into copies of his recent *Nation* magazine article entitled "Toward a World Parliament."

We don't know whether or not we are breaking any rules by standing near the entrance handing out this literature to the thousand people who have filed into the building. Dressed respectably as we are, me in my new Punjabi dress and Dick in the sport jacket he paid to have pressed by the hotel staff, we look very official. People seem to think we *are* the program. They even come up and ask when the plenary will begin. Best of all, a thousand people sit in chairs with little else to do except read our literature while they wait for the program to begin. Ganesh must have had a hand in this.

When the speakers finally *do* arrive, the sound system is so bad that it is impossible to decipher more than two words per sentence. Besides the abominable acoustics, there are other listening challenges. In the street outside passes a continuous procession of demonstrations, people shouting, chanting, drumming, and singing. Sometimes the demonstrators enter the building and march across the front of the stage with the speakers and the audience cheering them on. Surely, no one has gleaned any information from this morning session other than whatever they read in our handouts. Our mission is therefore more than adequately accomplished, so I convince Dick to leave early. I want to get some flip charts for the citizen-input session.

* * * *

It had crossed my mind when I introduced the idea of flip charts that I really had no idea where to get such a thing. I had seen some at Mr. Chavan's farmhouse classroom in Aurangabad, so I had assumed they could be bought in India.

"I wonder where to get flip charts," I call to Dick as we nudge our way through a logjam of revelers in the streets outside. I grab his arm to keep from losing him in the crowd. The atmosphere is like Mardi Gras in New Orleans, the crush of people, the colorful native costumes, the bands, the noise. Both sides of the narrow, crowded street are lined with bright banners promoting every imaginable progressive cause, *STOP FORCED EVICTIONS—FAIR TRADE, NOT FREE TRADE—STOP IMPERIALIST GLOBALIZATION.*

*Streets at the Goregaon Conference Grounds during
The World Social Forum.*

"We could try the press office,' says Dick. He checks his map and steers us slowly to a big quonset hut with one small door. A blonde young man guarding the entrance asks to see our press credentials. "We are looking for flip charts," I explain. "We need them to conduct a workshop in the forum."

"Not here. Try the information booth." He waves us on down the street.

The woman at the information table isn't much help either. "We need flip charts," I explain.

"What?" She gives me a quizzical look.

"Flip charts, large sheets of white paper to conduct a seminar, teach a class." I circumscribe a big rectangle with my hands.

The woman gestures toward the entrance. "Outside she says. By train station. One mile."

As we walk toward the Goregaon train station, we conclude that the woman at the information counter has given us a bum steer. This does not seem to be a shopping venue for conference visual aids. Rather it is a semi-rural slum neighborhood strewn with chicken wire and pieces of straw floating in puddles of stagnant water. Merchandise sold in stalls along the dirt pathway is limited to the hardware category of used pipes, nails, and rusty wire. I notice a stack of collapsed cardboard boxes that, by some stretch of the imagination, might serve as flip charts and consider buying them, but Dick says, "Let's ask someone back at the hotel this evening."

I agree. With more than a thousand seminars and workshops being offered here by people from all over the world, someone must have flip charts.

CHAPTER 21

Ganesh Removes All Obstacles

Although I'm told the maid will make our bed, I do it anyway. It helps me feel organized and provides a flat surface on which to lay out my things for our busy day of workshops. I'm so afraid of forgetting or losing something among the crowds.

First I lay out the small black backpack, so inseparable from my body. It isn't going to hold everything. Some things will have to be cradled in my arms.

Into the pack goes a stack of Andy's articles and a pad of lined paper to make a sign-in sheet. These are the bare essentials.

What else? Oh yes, the dupatta! The pretty blue dress and pants look great on me. Why this extraneous yardage? What a nuisance it was to haul around yesterday trying to keep it from dragging in the dust. By mid-morning, I had folded it up and stuffed it in my pack. I would like to leave it behind, but Sushama and Schweda had mentioned they might come to our workshops today and want to take my picture in this Indian garb. I fold the dupatta back into its cellophane wrapper and store it in the pack.

Next, the hard won flip charts. After asking everyone I met in the hotel whether anyone knew where to get them, the concierge had sent around their car last night to take me to a stationery store near the University. There I was able to acquire ten sheets of white paper measuring about three feet by four feet at a cost of three rupees each. A couple of felt tipped marker pens cost another ten rupees. However, later the car trip had appeared on our hotel bill at a cost of eight hundred rupees, nearly twenty dollars. Expensive flip charts!

The flip charts won't fit in the pack, so I roll them up into a huge cylinder which I tie together with a shoestring.

I also pack my handsome tan sweater with the grayish leaf pattern woven through, the one I had purchased in Kota. We will be at the conference center until well after dark and may have to come back in the draft of an auto rickshaw. I toss in a banana filched from the breakfast buffet as well as a leftover jelly sandwich wrapped in a piece of newspaper. There may not be time to stop for lunch.

Dick comes in to say the bus has arrived to take us to the conference center. "Have you forgotten anything?" he asks as we ride the balloon-like elevator down to the lobby.

"I hope not."

"Do you have some pens and a sign-in sheet?"

"Yes. I have put them in with my diary and the felt tipped pens."

"Is your diary in your backpack?"

"Yes, as always."

I murmur another prayer to Ganesh and trust that Schweda is also putting in a good word to him for us this morning.

* * * *

Our seminar room is one of the hundreds of temporary buildings that had been constructed at Gorgaon for the World Social Forum and they are marvels of Indian ingenuity. I have no idea where they found so many rough cut poles perhaps twenty feet in length and only two inches thick or how they stripped so many long sticks of their bark. But I have seen trucks on the road carrying enormous bundles of these and wondered where they had come from and where they would end up.

To construct this conference room for about fifty to a hundred people, they had to stand some of the poles erect and brace them with others at various angles, then stretch between them yards and yards of unbleached muslin. The ceilings are made of particle board which has been externally wired with fluorescent lights and ceiling fans.

We have no microphone. We will project our voices. Luckily our building is off in a remote part of the conference grounds away from the main flow of noisy demonstrators and the beating of drums. We have no idea how many people will attend. Hopefully most of the panel speakers will show up. Those are the people we want on the steering committee of our new coalition.

Noticing that the room is a little bare and lacks color, I remove from my pack the beautiful blue dupatta and drape it over the speakers' table. Its shiny gold trim frames the table nicely. The room is a little drafty this morning, so I take out my sweater and drape it over the back of one of the chairs in the last row. That will save my place while I go about my business signing people in, passing out flyers, greeting participants. As for the meeting itself, my contribution will be at the very beginning, introducing Andy as our keynote speaker. I will tell my favorite story of how I met him at the Hague Appeal for Peace in 1999, about the articles he has published ever since.

We are having a great time! People pour in from all over the world and introduce themselves by names we have seen only on the Internet. We know many of them well by their words and thoughts, but have never met them in person. There is Rasmus Tenbergen and his friend Fabian from Germany. They have an Internet web site called www.world-democracy.org that the future coalition can use for voting and organizing. There is Didier Coeurnelle from Belgium and Michael Nordfors from Norway as well as Mr. Antaryan and, of course, Mr. Chavan from India. A young man enters and I recognize him instantly even though I have never met him face to face nor ever seen his photo. Something in his manner says he must be Troy Davis with whom we have corresponded for many years. He is the son of Gary Davis, famous in our movement for dedicating his life at great sacrifice to the cause of global citizenship. Somehow Troy recognizes me as well, and we spontaneously hug one another like old friends.

The panel discussion goes on for hours with no one getting bored. Our three hours have passed followed by half the lunch hour when I suddenly recall that our citizen input session is supposed to

begin in half an hour on the other side of the conference grounds. I
interrupt Dick who is still moderating the panel and tell him I'm off
to put up the sign on the other building and get set up. I grab my
pack, grateful that it still contains the banana and jelly sandwich
left from breakfast. Hopefully, the rest of our core group, especially
Rob and Biplov who are supposed to be my first hour recorders,
will tear themselves away from the discussion and come along soon.

* * * *

The citizen input session is enormously popular. We start with
only a handful of people, but the room fills up gradually as the
minutes pass. There must be more than a hundred here now. My
voice holds up pretty well despite hours of shouting at the top of
my lungs. I'm on at least my dozenth cough drop.

This job is fairly easy. All I have to do is paraphrase, Rogerian
like, whatever anyone says and make sure Rob and Biplov get it
written down before the next point is made. Paraphrasing peoples'
thoughts is second nature, a lot like the counseling job I did for so
many years. The only problem here is to keep any one person from
monopolizing the floor for too long. I think the main reason people
come to meetings like this is because they want an audience. The
World Social Forum is, in one sense, a big *Speakers' Corner* like in
London. Most remarkable, however is that people at this workshop
keep to the subject and have given a lot of thought to the notion of
global democracy.

Rob and Biplov have been filling up the flip charts which they
have pinned to the muslin walls with safety pins from the clothing
repair kit I always keep in the bottom of my pack. Still the stiff,
cumbersome paper keeps falling off the walls, and the safety pins
are bent and crooked. Every so often Rob or Biplov stops to suck a
pricked finger. No one has offered to relieve them of their duty, so
they just keep writing.

When our three hours are up, people don't seem anxious to leave.
However, another group waiting outside has been scheduled for the
room at three o'clock, so we have to insist our time is up and practically chase people away. Dick makes sure everyone signs the roster
before they leave and gives them a copy of the schedule of our other
workshops.

I gather up the flip charts, roll them up again and secure them with the shoe string. Then I remember my sweater and dupatta. The dupatta had still been in use as a cloth for the speakers' table when I hurried out of the panel discussion at noon. By some miracle, it may still be there. It seems unlikely, however, that my sweater will still be on the back of the chair, what with a hundred thousand people milling about the conference grounds.

While Dick caucuses with Andy, Rob, and the rest of our core group, I muddle through the teeming crowds all the way back to our morning meeting room on the opposite side of the conference grounds. To my amazement, the dupatta is still there, inconspicuously disguised as a table cloth. The backs of all the chairs, however, are empty. A pity to lose the sweater I bought in Kota. It was such a useful garment and one of my favorite souvenirs of India.

* * * *

It has been a long week of successful organizing. Dick is down in the hotel parking garage disassembling our tandem bicycle to pack it back into the suitcase. We will check it on our plane to Seattle in the morning. Our two month journey into the dusty truth of India is over.

I feel positively wrung out as my limp body slumps into a chair in the computer room at the Intercontinental Hotel typing the notes that will go out by email to our old and new friends around the world.

It was on this very spot a few days ago that the strangest coincidence—or was it an answered prayer?—happened to me. After our citizen input session, I had come up here to type in Rob and Biplov's written words from the flip charts. The roll of charts was tucked, like a baton, under my arm as it had been much of the day. When I released the slipknot on the string that held them together, the paper automatically unrolled, making a slapping sound against the chair. At that moment, the tan sweater I had bought at the Kota market fell to the floor.

Needless to say, this startled me. A few hours earlier, I had gone to look for the sweater on the back of the conference room chair where I had recalled seeing it last. Because, it was not there,

I had concluded that I would never see it again. It had no doubt been found and claimed by one of the thousands of strangers attending the forum. But, impossible as this may seem, here it was on the floor at the foot of my chair about fifteen kilometers away across the teeming city of Bombay. Why?

The only explanation I could imagine was that I must have unconsciously taken the sweater with me to the citizen input session without realizing it, engrossed as I had been in what I was doing, Then, later on, without thinking of it still, I must have unconsciously rolled it up with the flip charts. It was scary to think I had done something like this without recalling it. As I have gotten older, my mind has started playing tricks on me, but this was, by far, the strangest.

The next morning, however, I learned the true explanation. I took the sweater with me to the morning session and placed it over the back of my chair as before. Soon Germa came in and pointed to it in surprise. "Where did you get that sweater?" he demanded.

I assumed he thought it a very unusual design, what with the gray leafy pattern knitted into the tan. "I bought it at the market in Kota," I answered casually.

"No! I mean where did you get it *today?* You see, yesterday I found that sweater on the back of a chair in the meeting room after everyone left the panel discussion. I thought it might belong to one of us, so I took it with me. Then I lost it again. Where did you find it?"

"I found it in the computer room when I went there last night to type up the notes from the flip charts," I said.

"Yes! That must have been where I left your sweater. I went to the computer room late yesterday afternoon to check my email. I must have dropped it by the chair."

I began to chuckle, then to laugh. "Oh, no! This is too strange. I thought I must have unconsciously rolled it up with the flip charts and then it fell out when I unrolled them in the computer room. I can't believe this!"

Germa and I looked at one another in astonishment and then had a hearty laugh together.

"That's an almost impossible coincidence," he said. "You must have a guardian angel looking after your clothes."

"Or a Hindu god, perhaps," I said.

I again smile at the memory as I write my final diary entry on our trip to India. It says,

> *We will spend our last night in India with the wonderful Indian family of our Servas hosts, Sushama and her daughter Schweda. I can hardly wait to tell Schweda how Ganesh, the elephant-faced god, has looked after us in answer to her prayers. He has helped us organize an international coalition to promote our dream of a world parliament elected by the people. In the meantime, he also kept track of my clothing.*

Printed in the United States
42428LVS00005B/295-306